T0168523

CUBA, HOT AND COLD

OTHER BOOKS BY TOM MILLER

PRAISE FOR TOM MILLER

TRADING WITH THE ENEMY

"Miller gives the reader a vivid sense of Cubans' endurance and inventiveness in dealing with surviving."

—*The Nation*

"May just be the best travel book about Cuba ever written."

—*Lonely Planet, Cuba*

"Tom Miller's book is written with wit and grace and is chock full of information that few, if any, know about Cuba. A wonderful book."

—*Jim Harrison*

THE PANAMA HAT TRAIL

"Part reportage, part travelogue, and all pleasure; it is written with enthusiasm and wit . . . filled with lively anecdotes, pungent asides, vivid scenes . . . a pleasure on every page of the journey."

—*Washington Post*

"Among the best travel books ever written."

—*National Geographic Traveler*

REVENGE OF THE SAGUARO

"[Miller is] a superb reporter and slyly funny stylist. This is a compulsively readable book by one of our best nonfiction writers."

—*San Francisco Chronicle*

CUBA, HOT AND COLD

TOM MILLER

THE UNIVERSITY OF
ARIZONA PRESS
TUCSON

The University of Arizona Press
www.uapress.arizona.edu

Printed in the United States of America
22   21   20   19   18   17   6   5   4   3   2   1

ISBN-13: 978-0-8165-3586-6 (paper)

Cover design by Leigh McDonald
Cover photos: *Taxi in Trinidad* [top] and *Sounds of Cuba* [bottom] by Bud Ellison

Library of Congress Cataloging-in-Publication Data
Names: Miller, Tom, 1947– author.
Title: Cuba, hot and cold / Tom Miller.
Description: Tucson : The University of Arizona Press, 2017. | Includes index.
Identifiers: LCCN 2017002332 | ISBN 9780816535866 (pbk. : alk. paper)
Subjects: LCSH: Cuba—Description and travel. | Cuba—Social life and customs. | Cuba—
    History. | Miller, Tom, 1947– —Travel—Cuba.
Classification: LCC F1788 .M477 2017 | DDC 972.91—dc23 LC record available at https://
    lccn.loc.gov/2017002332

♾ This paper meets the requirements of ANSI/NISO Z39.48-1992 (Permanence of Paper).

To the next generation of Albarráns:

Noel, Lucas, Marcos, and Lola

CONTENTS

ACKNOWLEDGMENTS

The following have been wonderfully helpful throughout: the Albarrán family here, there, and everywhere; Mike Miller; Paquito Vives; my *compañero literario* Jesús Vega; Janis Lewin; and Joann Biondi.

CUBA, HOT AND COLD

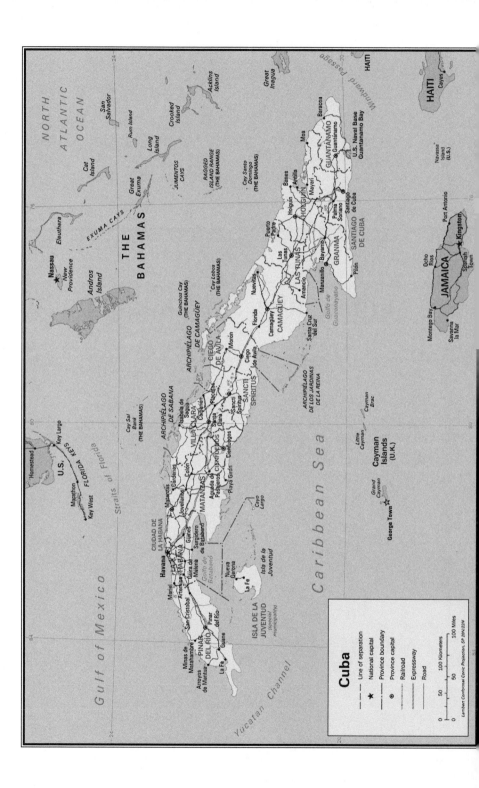

INTRODUCTION

"I want to get there before it changes."

If I heard that once I heard it five hundred times. The speakers were invariably middle-class Americans who, having learned that diplomatic relations between Cuba and the United States were warming, hoped to see Havana and the rest of the country in its pre-McDonald's mode. In short, before capitalism overran communism.

Before it changes? You don't understand. *You are the change*, dear reader, *you are the change*.

Nostalgia for old American clunkers? To get misty-eyed for classic American cars is to long for the embargo, because that's the only reason those cars are there. When you see chauffeur-driven vintage American convertibles tooling down the Malecón with smiling tourists in the backseats waving to impoverished Cubans on the nearby sidewalk, well, that's only one step away from occupiers acknowledging the occupied.

Take your time, chicos and chicas. The change you want to precede isn't going to take place anytime soon.

My travels through Cuba, lasting from a few days to many months, took place during the Special Period in a Time of Peace, a euphemism for the island's economic free fall. Although the Cold War was over and done with elsewhere, U.S. foreign policy ensured years of convoluted change when nothing in Cuba was available all the time. I wrote occasional accounts of Cuban life in that era, and now, looking back on it, I see a pattern. Without realizing it, I was there before the change.

In those days, right-wing first-wave Cubans in America discouraged visits and even phone calls between the two countries. Isolation was the attitude of the day.

Back in those dark ages, communication between the United States and Cuba was extremely difficult. Few Cubans had home phones, and fewer of those functioned adequately. Neighbors used neighbors' phones all the time. When I wanted to arrange a call to Cuba I'd either send a telegram a few days early suggesting the time and number I'd call, or I'd use a gray-market operator in Canada who, at an agreed-upon time, would link my phone line with a Cuban line, allowing a third-country conversation to take place. The Canadian would bill me for both calls and add a service charge. And mail service? Ha! It often took four or more weeks for a letter to get to Cuba, and you were lucky if it actually reached its destination, To add insult to injury, because there were no relations between the two neighbors, mail had to go through a third country (i.e., Mexico). Is it any wonder that the only safe and secure way to send a letter to Cuba was to have a traveling friend hand-deliver it?

I had breakfast one morning in 1990 with a Miami-based journalist who had to leave for the States early. She handed me a short stack of envelopes, all neatly addressed; could I deliver these letters? A day or so later I found myself in Barrio Chino and realized that one of the letters was addressed to a woman there. I knocked on the door, Regla Albarrán answered it, and two and a half years later we were married.

The Cold War carried on, and the U.S. government hoped to learn what it could about Cuba's economy through old-fashioned spying. They wanted to know the availability of crops at neighborhood *mercados* and how the day-to-day produce supply was holding up. Most workers at the U.S. Interests Section—our embassy that wasn't an embassy—lived in Miramar and discussed the availability of household goods. Diplomats were allowed to shop at the Diplotienda, a supermarket for foreigners; even U.S. Marines who lived in a complex on Seventh Avenue were allowed to shop there. Because I was integrated into Cuban society and traveled through the country with some ease, the CIA tried to recruit me.

But not for the first time. That was back in the winter of 1968 when, at age twenty-one, I worked for a news agency in Washington, D.C. We covered college news, the anti–Vietnam War movement, and occasionally student movements overseas. Now and then we'd get phone calls from readers wanting details beyond the stories. One man who expressed interest invited me for dinner at a walk-down Dupont Circle Chinese restaurant. He explained that his organization was looking for a young American journalist to travel through Latin America filing reports about student movements. They'd cover my expenses, I'd be enrolled in Spanish courses, I could visit my brother— then a Peace Corpsman in South America—and I would be free to sell these stories to any publication I wanted, as long as I faithfully filed stories on Latin American student movements with him and his unnamed organization. The fellow was very suspect. He operated an African art gallery but asked that I not meet him there. Once he paid for our dinner, I never heard from him again.

Attempt number two: not long after I moved to Havana for a long stretch I met a fellow from the U.S. Interests Section. I innocently asked him if I could receive mail from the States at his office because regular mail took so long to get to Cuba. He allowed as how this might be possible if I were to be cooperative regarding his inquiries about the country. I dropped the subject and continued to get my mail the usual delayed way.

Attempt number three: I received a call in my Tucson office one day in this century's first decade from a fellow who, unlike the others, made it clear he worked for the CIA. They had been reading some of my published reports from Cuba; would I be amenable to visiting their headquarters in D.C. to talk with him and his colleagues about

Cuba? I was utterly taken aback, speechless, incredulous. *Me asustó.* I regained my composure. "Go on," I said. "We'll cover your airfare and lodging, of course." "Mm-hmm," I replied. "And you'll receive an honorarium of five hundred dollars." At this I laid down the phone and slapped my cheek. The CIA thought I was worth only five hundred dollars? *Puh-leeze.*

I declined, telling him that anything I had to say to the CIA they could read in my books. And so, dear reader, what follows is for you, your neighbors, and the CIA.

CUBANA BE, CUBANA BOP

I'm listening to "Cubana Be, Cubana Bop" right now, Dizzy Gillespie's terrific 1947 musical alloy of traditional jazz, Latin rhythms, intricate drumming, and Afro-Cuban chanting. The mix of American jazz with muscular, otherworldly sounds gave us something altogether fresh, simultaneously rough and sophisticated, captivating and unique—much as foreigners have seen Cuba in the intervening decades.

When the U.S. government broadened the definition of who could legally travel to Cuba in the late 1990s, an overflow of applications came gushing in. While the number of American tourists ignoring U.S. strictures on travel to the island continued to increase, a whole new breed started to appear: "study groups." My favorite was a flock of undergraduate English majors from a frost-belt college who came to the sunny Caribbean in the dead of winter. They were the usual bunch—unfailingly polite, hair adolescent orange, and hopelessly monolingual. They were in Cuba, they averred, to learn about Hemingway in Havana. And this is how these American college students studied Hemingway in Havana: every morning after finishing their hotel's breakfast buffet, they returned to their rooms, changed into their swimsuits, picked up a towel and a Hemingway paperback or two, and descended to the pool, where they lay down in lounge chairs to study Hemingway in Havana.

By the time Raúl Castro and Barack Obama announced rapprochement, most Americans had softened to allowing Cuba into their family of friends. This attitude didn't just appear overnight; a number of events, mostly nonpolitical, had to take place first. One was baseball. In the spring of 1999 the Baltimore Orioles, after months of negotiating, traveled to Cuba for a game against Cuba's best. I wasn't a huge fan of Fidel Castro's, but to see him emerge from the home team dugout with the Cuban lineup card and lumber across the infield to hand it over to the umpires before some 45,000 fans at the Latin American Stadium, well, I got all choked up. Both countries' flags rose above center field and the two national anthems played—in our case, what seemed to be an old, scratchy 78-rpm rendition of "The Star Spangled Banner." Fidel took his box seat behind home plate next to the then baseball commissioner Bud Selig and they watched the Orioles beat Cuba, 3–2.

The visit by Pope John Paul II contributed to the rinsing away of hostilities. "Let Cuba open itself to the world," the Pope implored, "and the world open itself to Cuba."

What made most Americans aware of Cuba, though, was the saga of Elián González, the tyke who survived a motorboat ride from Cuba. Elián was placed in the custody of distant relatives in Miami despite the wishes of his father, who remained in Cuba. The Elián saga tore apart the Cuban American community while the rest of the country watched the boy treated as political bait. Beyond South Florida's Cuban American community, there was relief when the kid was eventually returned to his father.

These three events—baseball, the Pope's visit, and the Elián González case—brought aspects of Cuba to Americans that went far beyond the embargo. Yet it was the improbable success of a handful of aging musicians that exposed a Cuba few knew and expanded the country's audiences far beyond its bashers or its cheerleaders. The musicians went by the name of the Buena Vista Social Club, their music came from the 1950s and earlier, and their appeal was resolutely apolitical. On a visit to Havana, the American musician and producer Ry Cooder, not finding the musicians he sought, instead teamed up with Cuban producer Juan de Marcos to produce an album of exquisite sounds from another era.

One of Cooder's Cuba visits coincided with Hurricane Irene, which stormed through Havana one night inundating streets near the coast and knocking down power poles throughout the city. In San Miguel del Padrón, a poor working-class suburb southeast of the capital, Juanito Rodríguez Peña and his wife, Marta, heard the torrential downpour and howling wind, warily took note of the water entering their hundred-year-old wood house, and went back to sleep. The high-ceilinged front room had a few merciless leaks, and the wind overturned the couple's only furniture—a straw chair and a wicker couch—yet in all they survived Irene better than most. The next morning the nimble guitar maker went to his backroom workshop, took the plastic sheet off an instrument he was working on, brushed huge puddles of water from his workbench let in by the porous roof, and began his day. Marta spent the morning sweeping water out the front door.

Juanito Rodríguez Peña had been making and playing guitars, *treses*, and lutes for much of his life. The *tres* is most succinctly described as a slightly smaller guitar with three sets of two strings each. The Cuban lute, commonly called a *laúd*, has a pear-shaped body, usually with eighteen strings. Rodríguez Peña, born in the nearby suburb of Luyanó more than seven decades earlier, had gained a measure of notoriety throughout Cuba for his regular appearances on the popular radio program *Vivimos en Campo Alegre* and the television show *Palmas y Cañas*. Both programs feature Rodríguez Peña's forte, *música guajira*—traditional acoustic music from the countryside. Rodríguez Peña performed around Havana frequently and, drawing on precariously few resources, made and repaired instruments. His raw materials appeared irregularly and sometimes serendipitously—much like the bus that carried him into town to rehearsals, studios, and performances. To follow the story of Juanito Rodríguez Peña and his survival is likewise to get a sense of Cuba today; it involves, in varying proportions, inventiveness, skill, resourcefulness, and occasional good fortune.

Rodríguez Peña's most recent good fortune began about four years prior to Irene. Among the astute musicians who have bought guitars from him was the late Compay Segundo, the nonagenarian Santiago de Cuba native who, with other elder statesmen of Cuban music, won a Grammy for his part in the Buena Vista Social Club ensemble. The music Segundo played came from the far end of the nineteenth century at the far end of the island.

During the initial Buena Vista recording session in 1996 Ry Cooder asked Segundo where his guitar came from. This was no idle chatter between musicians. There was something about Segundo's guitar that piqued Cooder's curiosity. As both producer and musician, Cooder has the admirable distinction of having strummed quality instruments throughout the world, and his recordings over the years reveal a man obsessed with perfection. If you're thinking about buying a guitar or a tres or a laúd in Havana, Segundo advised, Juanito Rodríguez Peña is your man. Two days later the guitar player from Southern California and the guitar maker from San Miguel del Padrón met, and right away the former bought two instruments from the latter: a reconditioned laúd originally made by Rodríguez Peña's father, Andrés, a guitar maker who died more than thirty years earlier, and a tres that Rodríguez Peña had converted from a *requinto*, a small similar instrument from Mexico. Cooder considered Rodríguez Peña a master craftsman. Rodríguez Peña thought of Cooder as a tall and amiable foreigner.

A year later Cooder asked Rodríguez Peña to build an instrument for him from scratch. "As a luthier he stands apart from any other string instrument maker I know," Cooder told me. "He is an Old World folk artist. Since there are no music stores per se in Cuba, one simply has to know of the makers. In America and Europe musicians have two or five or dozens of their own instruments. In Cuba, you have one. Musicians bring their battered instruments to Rodríguez Peña and he makes chicken soup from stones. His guitars tell a certain story when you play them. There's something about how he positions the neck, how he frets an instrument. I look for the joinery and the woodworking, the angle of the neck where it joins the body, the height of the strings at the bridge, the setup of the stress points. That's what determines how it sounds. It's what makes a Stradivarius a Stradivarius."

A visit to Rodríguez Peña's workshop can be disorienting. I expected to see the mild disarray of a carpenter, with tools of his trade, stacks of wood, and sawdust lying about. Instead I was confronted by an almost barren workspace. The only objects in sight were a small throw rug, a handsaw, an almost empty can of 90 percent cane alcohol, and a Stanley electric saw. "I haven't tried it in a long time," Rodríguez Peña told me. "I'm not sure it works." A single fluorescent light hanging from the ceiling illuminated more spiderwebs than guitars. Additional light shone through the windows and great gaps in the roof. The front panel of an old stand-up bass rested against a far wall. "It comes from Luyanó. I haven't decided what to do with it yet," he explained. Rodríguez Peña has lived in this house since 1939, and it was right here that as a young boy he would sit in the corner and watch his dad at work.

"My father's workshop used to extend a little farther out. He would make furniture and doors as well as instruments. Eventually he devoted himself to the luthier trade. He allowed me to cut wood sometimes, but I couldn't use his electric sander. He was proud of me, but he never let me make instruments by myself. The parents of that era were real strict. Domineering." Rodríguez Peña turned his fist as if tightening a faucet. "I really didn't begin my work until he died."

Rodríguez Peña had few supplies but a world of suppliers. He had no tools to calibrate depth or measure width, yet by eyeballing the wood his pieces fit snugly together. Somewhat by happenstance my family found itself in the middle of a typical Cuban problem and its typically Cuban solution. My wife, Regla, was visiting her father, a retired Havana carpenter, and dropped in, on my behalf, to see Rodríguez Peña. The guitar maker told her in passing that he needed a particular type of lacquer for his work. Regla mentioned this to her father, who allowed as how he had some of that lacquer he no longer used. She relayed this news to Rodríguez Peña, who, the next day, rode the bus to my father-in-law's. The two elderly woodworkers chewed the fat for a while, and Rodríguez Peña got his lacquer.

Fulfilling Rodríguez Peña's professional needs is usually not so easy, but he does rely a lot on friendships. As a licensed independent craftsman he could get wood from the government, but it never seems to be the right type or age. For many years carpenter and luthier friends would simply give him planks of wood. Or he would go scavenging, traipsing through sites where the ruins of once-splendid homes might offer up the right wood. Sometimes he'd explore the trash that builds up on the streets of Luyanó. Such excursions are now rare for Rodríguez Peña, who when I met him had just celebrated his seventy-first birthday, but on an unseasonably muggy winter afternoon he and I accompanied one of his suppliers, forty-two-year-old guitar maker Luis García, on his wood-hunting rounds.

———

García, who learned guitar making from a Mexican master, lives on the first floor of an enormous apartment building across the street from a cigarette plant and a bicycle repair shop. "I made guitars in a factory," García says as we pull away from the curb and drive by the nearby baseball stadium, "but I didn't like the production-line work." He directs our driver down potholed side streets in the Cerro neighborhood. "Pull over there," he instructs, pointing toward a narrow street. "Sometimes there's a trash pile on the far side." Havana's anguished efforts to keep up with itself mean fewer trash pickups, hence more and bigger trash piles. This can be good if you're dumpster diving for wood, but at this particular corner, after walking the perimeter of the junk heap, García and Rodríguez Peña both shake their heads. "I go out looking just about every evening after dinner," García explains as we get moving again, "either on foot or bicycle. Often I don't get home until midnight. I stop to visit friends and family. In the last six years I've found six complete mahogany beds. I hardly ever skip a night. If you miss a night you might miss a bed. Let's try over there."

Scavengers are either trash collectors or object hunters, author Paul Auster observes in *In the Country of Last Things*. "A good object hunter," notes Auster, "must be quick, you must be clever, and you must know where to look." García agrees with Auster: "What another has seen fit to throw away"—Auster again—"you must examine, dissect, and bring back to life."

The trash pile García points to on the corner looks more promising, and we all climb out. Across the street sits a once-lovely building now in the final stages of decay. Its Greek columns lay prostrate and broken on the ground, and chunks of concrete dot the rubble. A dog barks from a third-floor window in a nearby building; children shoot marbles on the corner. García reaches carefully into the pile and pulls out a flat piece of dry wood about three feet by four feet and hands it to Rodríguez Peña. "Rosewood," the master craftsman says, tapping it as he holds it up to his ear. He runs his hand over it and taps it again. "Rosewood," he repeats. "Too new. New wood is no good. It has to be forty or fifty years old." A few blocks away we stop again and find another piece. Rodríguez Peña lifts it to gauge its heft. "Nails. It's got nails in it. It won't do."

"See that corner?" García asks. "One night I found a piano top there. Another night I found some furniture. It's my best place. I always check it out." Yet by the end of our hunt all we've collected is a warning from a traffic cop for drifting slightly over the center white line.

One evening not long thereafter, Rodríguez Peña, laúd in hand, traveled by bus into Havana with his wife, Marta, to perform with his group, JRP, at a cultural center in the heart of town. Juanito's five-man group attracted upward of a hundred appreciative spectators, including the tall foreigner and his wife. Many in the audience were themselves from the countryside, and this was one of the few opportunities they had in the city to comfortably connect with their culture and see live música guajira. Rodríguez Peña, his thin five-foot-ten frame clad in a freshly pressed guayabera and dark slacks, played the laúd, an instrument as refined in sound as it is in verse. The late Andalusian poet Rafael Alberti used the laúd in metaphoric verse to set the migration from North Africa to Spain and on to the New World. "In the beginning was the laúd," his poem "Invitation to a Sonorous Voyage" begins. His poet's-eye view of history describes the breakup of the Spanish empire: laúds "ignite their bridges in sparks of gold, along the stars that Spain has lost."

It's the instrument that ignited Efraín Amador, a Cuban who has devoted his life to the laúd and tres as both composer and performer. Amador, his country's leading authority on the two instruments, has strummed Bach, Beethoven, and Mozart on the laúd in concerts throughout Europe, Africa, and the Americas with his wife accompanying him on the piano. "It took me years to convince the Instituto Superior de Arte here that these weren't just some hillbilly instruments," the fifty-three-year-old told me in his home in Guanabacoa, outside Havana, "that they deserved to be studied alongside the piano and violin." In the late 1980s the laúd and tres got official approval, and Amador is now their champion. His personal collection includes a laúd from Rodríguez Peña.

Six months after Cooder ordered his instrument Rodríguez Peña had given it a lot of thought but not much time. Although Cooder has become associated worldwide with Cuban music through the success of the Buena Vista Social Club, in Cuba itself radio did not play songs from the CD, stores did not stock it, and, with the exception of a few special screenings, theaters had not shown the film. The guitar maker, clueless to the Buena Vista album or its producer's identity, continued to refer to Cooder simply as "the tall foreigner."

When Cooder next visited Rodríguez Peña he brought along enough wood for his own instrument and plenty more, and enough lacquer and glue to build and recondition a dozen used instruments. "¡Que bárbaro!" Rodríguez Peña cried out when he saw the gifts. "Outrageous!" It was a reunion of sorts, and the player and the maker hugged warmly. Rodríguez Peña picked up a sheet of Alaskan Sitka spruce from Cooder and tapped it next to his ear, listening for its resonance. He did this often, testing the wood with the intense wonderment of a child. "Hear that?" he said, holding it next to my ear. Actually, I didn't hear what the master guitar maker heard, but I did see the gleam in his eye. Rodríguez Peña and the tall foreigner talked about the pending construction of the instrument, a tres. Neither the world-class guitarist nor the world-class luthier spoke the other's language, but they chatted amiably about the tres with very little help from a third party.

"In the modern era of guitar making you may have master craftsmen," Cooder said later, "but a number of different specialists' hands work on the same instrument. Rarely do you find a shop where one maker works on one instrument from start to finish. You simply can't get instruments like this anymore, not in the competitive marketplace. Rodríguez Peña doesn't work in the contemporary commercial environment, so he can make the effort to bring forth the best. We live in an era of technical proficiency, but this goes far beyond that. You could not replicate an instrument from him in New York, London, or Los Angeles."

Cooder returned to Rodríguez Peña's modest home the next day, not to further his tres but for a lesson on the laúd. With the master and the teacher at work, it hardly mattered that they come from very different backgrounds and occupy extremely different stations in life, or that neither of them reads sheet music. Cooder was learning to play the "Zapateo Cubano," and Rodríguez Peña was showing him on his own laúd how best to position his hands. Never have I seen twenty such educated fingers at play. A day later Rodríguez Peña unlocked an old tobacco-scented armoire in the bedroom and showed me where he keeps two of his own instruments. Then he pulled away a blanket on a table to reveal two more he is working on. After that he took me over to a bookshelf and uncovered yet two more. Most of his instruments were safely stored in the house's only room with no overhead leaks. Finally he escorted me out through the workshop to his narrow backyard. We passed by a painting of Rodríguez Peña's younger brother Orlando, whose death in a traffic accident some twenty-five years earlier still brought sorrow to his usually cheerful face.

"As soon as I finish that tres I'll build a new cinderblock workshop," he announced, designing his new workplace with his hands. The backyard, where Marta hung clothes to dry, yielded bananas, mangoes, guayaba, and frutabomba, and their sweet aroma wafted through the house. A pig Rodríguez Peña was fattening up for the family's Christmas fiesta snorfed by, and the guitar maker drew a hand across his throat and smiled.

The laúd teacher still beamed from the previous day's lesson. "The foreigner learned the 'Zapateo' in its entirety! It was in 6/8 time. He's extremely talented and intelligent. He has an excellent sense of rhythm. What did you say his name is?"

When we passed back through the bedroom, I noticed a Bible open to the Book of Luke next to some plastic flowers. Rodríguez Peña goes to Pentecostal meetings where they sing and talk about God. "It's every Wednesday night for an hour or so. With all my music and guitar making, I haven't had much time for it lately." Rodríguez Peña has been a member of Cuba's Communist Party for more than twenty years. "We had a study session last Saturday," he said of his party chapter. "We discussed the problems of the revolution and read some of the country's laws." Likewise, he serves on the neighborhood

Committee for the Defense of the Revolution. "We keep the streets clean. It's volunteer revolutionary work. We paint the curbs. We discuss neighborhood problems at our meetings."

A couple of evenings later I was chatting with Rodríguez Peña and his wife in their daughter's house, just across the street from their own, when the electricity suddenly shut down throughout the neighborhood. It was time for the weekly two-hour blackout. I commiserated with them about this hardship, but almost as one the entire family rose to contradict me. "No, don't you see? We used to have blackouts every day for hours at a time. Things are getting back to normal."

Rodríguez Peña stood on his daughter's front porch and plucked out a riff on his tres. The next day he would ask local municipal officials for a permit to patch up his hurricane-damaged roof with wood and corrugated metal he hoped to find. On the way he planned to stop at the bank to pay his monthly eighty-peso license fee to maintain an independent repair shop. He assured me he will get to the tall foreigner's tres as soon as things are in order.

———

I maintain that it was the phenomenon of the Buena Vista Social Club—its worldwide concert tour, German cineaste Wim Wenders's documentary film, and of course its albums—that ultimately eased relations between the two countries and made backdoor diplomacy more possible. The last survivor of the original group was singer Omara Portuondo, the only one of the bunch who could rightly claim individual fame exclusive of the others. Born in 1930 during the growing tumult of the dictator Geraldo Machado's regime, Portuondo became an international sensation partly because of her enduring showmanship and partly because of her good fortune in having been knighted into the realm of the Buena Vista Social Club. Over the years she became as well known in her home country as Barbra Streisand was in hers. The Buena Vista album Portuondo sang on sold 1.1

million copies and won a Grammy in 1998. The film received an Oscar nomination.

After the group's enormously successful performances Portuondo toured the States, this time as the headliner. She appeared in Los Angeles with Barbarito Torres, a laúd player, then returned to Hollywood for a salsa and Latin jazz festival. We spoke in the middle of this tour.

Her voice sounded stronger as a solo act, I said, than it had been the previous year when she was part of the Buena Vista ensemble. She considered this and agreed, adding, "It's etiquette. I was one element in a larger show. This time it's my show, and I don't have those restrictions."

Havana's Cabaret Tropicana has always been Portuondo's home. Best known for its revue of high-kicking and great-looking dancers in revealing glittery costumes, the Tropicana also has showcased major Cuban singing talent. It was there at the end of World War II that a shy fifteen-year-old Portuondo would watch her sister Haydée rehearse. One day the troupe needed a last-minute replacement, and Omara filled in.

"I love the Tropicana. I have a permanent invitation to perform there. I opened for Nat 'King' Cole at the Tropicana and introduced him. He impressed me so much; he was a lovely black man in a white suit." Portuondo broke into "Unforgettable," imitating Cole for a few lines. She also recalled Tony Bennett at the pre-Castro Tropicana and at the Sans Souci. "I saw Sarah Vaughan, too, but I never sang with her. She was wonderful."

Big-band music from the United States inspired Portuondo and other Cuban musicians back then. "Glenn Miller and also the Dorsey brothers influenced our music, including boleros, a mix that gave birth to *filin*," a soft, crooning romantic style that achieved its peak popularity in the 1950s. "The cha-cha-chá was also influenced by North American music, and so was Pérez Prado and the mambo."

Although Portuondo is anything but political, historical events helped shape her career. She was performing in Florida with her sister when the October 1962 Cuban Missile Crisis erupted. She returned home; Haydée remained. Because so many entertainers in the following years preferred life abroad and far fewer foreigners performed in Cuba, it was easier for those who stayed, Portuondo among them, to advance their careers.

Yet just when her solo career was to be launched in October 1967, the death of revolutionary Che Guevara in Bolivia sent the nation into official mourning and closed the nightclubs for a spell. Then, in 1970, when Fidel Castro exhorted the nation to produce ten million tons of sugar cane, troupes from the Tropicana, including Portuondo, and other cultural institutions, such as the Ballet Nacional, traveled the countryside entertaining the cane cutters.

I have a theory, I told her, that the U.S. embargo has actually helped Cuban culture, that its authenticity owes its preservation, in part, to U.S. foreign policy.

Portuondo's answer turned my statement inside out.

"That's true, but it wasn't North American foreign policy. It was what we did at home. After the triumph of the revolution, the new Ministry of Culture made a sweeping effort to rescue all the different cultures from throughout the island. They established *casas de cultura* in every province, trained art instructors, created new ballet schools and folkloric groups, and gave free classes. That's what preserved our culture. I taught popular Cuban dance for a while after the revolution."

Portuondo, who has been compared with Billie Holiday and Edith Piaf in their primes, had recently released an album for her North American tour. "A lot of Latinos come to my shows," she said with respect and surprise. "The Latinos join in the singing and clapping, and they dance in the aisles."

Portuondo moves about on stage as if leading an aerobics class. A British newspaper complimented her "regal presence, accentuated by a considerable sexual magnetism." Her fingers are long and narrow, her mocha skin as smooth as the Caribbean the day after a hurricane.

Musical director Jesús "Aguaje" Ramos, who led Omara's onstage band of some dozen musicians, playfully refers to her as "*la más sexi*," a nickname he encourages the audience to call out as well. "I'm not sure if I'm *la sexi diva*," she later mischievously confessed, "or *la diva sexi*."

Earlier that day I pulled out a thirty-year-old record album of hers I'd bought from a sidewalk vendor in Havana the previous year for a dollar, and she went through it commenting on each arrangement and songwriter. Then I produced a 1990 CD of hers that shows her wearing an Afro that was, frankly, not flattering.

"But I don't use anything artificial in my hair and I never have, not even a straightener. Look. It's all mine." And with that she suddenly yanked off the elastic band that had kept her hair in a neat bun and unleashed her lush, black hair in two thick rolls as if creating a V. Each hand held one roll, extended to their fullest high above her head. "See?"

I also produced a picture of her father, taken when he was a star infielder for Almendares, one of two perennially popular Havana baseball teams. Like many Cuban standouts, Bartolo Portuondo played in the Negro National League in the States after its founding in 1920. "Look!" she cried out to her son Ariel, who served as her road manager. "It's your grandfather!" He led the Cuban league in stolen bases one year, and he played for the home team when an American squad starring Babe Ruth barnstormed through the island. "I used to go see my dad play at the Tropical stadium. He became a coach after his playing days were over."

To Portuondo, who has performed with popular Cuban groups ranging from Cuarteto Las D'Aida in the 1950s to the contemporary NG La Banda, there is no one "golden age" of Cuban music. "It's cyclical," she said, moving her arms in a wide circle. "There have been various moments of gold in Cuban music. We're at the top of the cycle again right now because we keep inventing as we draw a lot from the past. The Buena Vista boom has been remarkable not only for those of us who are part of it but for all *orquestas* that play this type of music.

"Our international schedules are so full it was only a couple of months ago that all of the Buena Vista Social Club could finally get together to play for the Cuban public. We performed at the Karl Marx Theater. We had a packed house with hundreds more in the streets. There were people of all ages. It was incredibly emotional." Their final show took place May 2016.

For all Portuondo's international travels and notoriety, what I found most revealing was not her stage show or the enthusiastic reception international audiences have given her. It was her wristwatch. It's always set to Havana time.

———

José Martí, leader of Cuba's nineteenth-century independence movement, is said to have had a voice that sounded like an oboe. Perhaps that's why the country has so many oboe players. I took oboe lessons in Havana when I lived there in the early 1990s and wrote about them at the time. I was hoping to improve my mediocre oboe skills acquired during junior high school, and frankly, I wanted to show readers that contemporary music in Cuba was more than just salsa and reggaeton. I succeeded with the latter, but far less with improving my ability. I even had trouble with the ducks in Prokofiev's *Peter and the Wolf*. And so I put my oboe on the top shelf in my Arizona office where it gathered desert dust. I'd glance up at it now and then with a sense of forlorn pride, reassuring myself that I owned a quality instrument that I once played with some gusto.

Dust gathered for some twenty-five years. At times I considered the instrument little more than a "dull black tube scattered with metal keys," as Blair Tindall describes her first oboe in *Mozart in the Jungle—Sex, Drugs, and Classical Music*. During those years I led literary tours of Havana and beyond. One autumn as I began organizing the following January's trip I looked up at the dust-encrusted oboe case and thought, if I leave it there another twenty-five years, half a century's dust will have accumulated and not one orchestra will ever have tuned to my oboe's A-above-middle-C, as is the global custom.

Back when Adlai Stevenson was the Democratic Party's standard-bearer my family lived across the street from an elementary school named for the Frenchman Lafayette; my parents were active in school affairs there. One of my earliest memories is a pile of musical instruments in the living room growing in size as parents dropped off unused instruments to be distributed among primary school children. I wished that pile still existed so I could donate my unused oboe. Instead, I packed it on my next trip to Cuba.

Whatever happened to my old oboe teacher in Havana, Jesús Avilés? He had, I learned, moved to the city of Matanzas, sixty-five miles east. In the capital he was the principal oboist for Cuba's Orquesta Sinfónia Nacional, but in Matanzas he taught oboe to eight students. I took my Literary Havana group to a publishing house in Matanzas one day and invited Jesús to join us afterward at the Velasco Hotel's dining room. (He was remarkably easy to find.) Before lunch I ceremoniously presented him with my old oboe and asked him to give it to a deserving student. There was a smattering of applause, and I surprised myself by getting all choked up for parting with a token of my youth. We were served a choice of pork or fish.

The oboe, made by the Robert Thibaud company in Paris, went not to a student right away but to Pedro Puentes, one of Havana's two woodwind repairmen. Pedro lived in Marianao, a suburb that foreigners see only on their way to the Tropicana Cabaret. He made double reeds for oboes, the oboe d'amore, English horns, and bassoons, and sold them for about a dollar each. Pedro overhauled my old Thibaud—tightening screws, adjusting pads and metal, replacing cork, and repairing slight leaks. "When Pedro finishes restoring it," Jesús said with quiet pride, "it will be good as new." Much of Marianao, on the other hand, was in worse shape than the worst oboe, strewn as it was with abundant potholes, cracked sidewalks, and homes in desperate need of rewiring, replumbing, repainting, and reconstruction. Marianao looked like no one had tended to it since Batista left Cuba.

Pedro led me to the small workbench in the second-floor bedroom to which the city's woodwind musicians brought their ailing instruments. His granddaughter, who lived with him and his wife, moistened a double reed, climbed up on the double bed, and tooted a couple of scales on her father's oboe. Her eight-year-old right pinky practically reached the low C, C#, and D# keys. "I don't want her to decide on the oboe at her age," Pedro said. "She should try other instruments as well."

The good-as-new Thibaud was now in the hands of Jesús, who started considering each of his students. Eventually he decided upon fourteen-year-old Lorena Gómez, who had been playing oboe since she was ten. Her qualifications: "Dedication. Ambition. Potential. Family support. A sweet tone comes out of her instrument. She wants to play oboe professionally."

Lorena, her parents, Jesús, and his wife met me at the bus when I next traveled to Matanzas. Jesús had recently suffered a severe bout of pneumothorax, more commonly known as collapsed lung. Two procedures at a Matanzas hospital were required to eliminate a bubble in one lung and to fix a perforation in the other. In all, he spent twenty days and zero pesos in the Faustino Pérez Hospital. By the time I reached Matanzas the good news was that Jesús was in full recovery mode. The unfortunate news was that his lungs could no longer generate sufficient air pressure to vibrate a reed and produce the oboe's tone. After more than fifty years playing the oboe throughout the Americas and Europe, sixty-eight-year-old Jesús Avilés's oboe-playing days were over. Sure, he could still teach—embouchure, fingering, posture—but he couldn't coax even a squeak out of his instrument.

The six of us walked a few blocks to the José White Concert Hall where Lorena set up her music stand on stage, put her moistened double reed in the oboe, and, alone with an audience of five, played an Albinoni oboe concerto. She stood about five-foot-four, dark hair, dark eyes, light skin, and a teen-age smile. She wore a pretty pink dress for the occasion.

Nicely played, we all agreed. She showed poise where she might have shown anxiety, composure where tension wouldn't have surprised us. "¿Ves?" Jesus motioned. "See?" We all congratulated her and walked over to a state-run snack bar on Parque de la Libertad. On the way we passed a recently established hot spot where giggling young *matanceros* tried out their smartphones for the first time. "You are all invited to lunch," Lorena's dad, Orlando, proclaimed to us all once we arrived at the snack bar. "We have plenty of shrimp at the house." Although a college grad, he chose to work at the Restaurante Italiano, part of the Meliá hotel complex at the nearby beach resort of Varadero. The tips were better than a government salary.

We took a cab to their home in Barrio Peñas Altas, climbed to the second floor of a duplex where their dog Sofi greeted us, and sat on the back porch with a lovely view of Matanzas Bay. While Orlando prepared lunch Lorena played a short piece on their painfully out of tune upright piano.

Each province has a music school named for a musician except, curiously, for the one Lorena attended in Matanzas. It was named for Alfonso Pérez Isaac, active in the Castro revolution and the Angolan War. The list of martyrs and the list of schools must not have come out even.

Lorena was soon to take a national exam to qualify for the music conservatory in Havana where they taught music theory. She'd play in ensemble groups there and learn how to whittle her own reeds. "The state supplies low-quality Chinese oboes and plastic ones." Jesús made a face. "She'll have no trouble getting into the Havana school with this new one." As a light rain fell we spent the afternoon taking pictures of each other and eating shrimp. We could hear freighters plying Matanzas Bay.

ON THE STREET

It's surprisingly easy to sidestep the well-marked tourist trail, to get under Cuba's skin. Spend forty centavos to ride a city bus. Pass an afternoon walking the streets of 10 de Octubre or La Lisa, two neighborhoods that seldom see foreigners. Late at night circle around back to Centro Habana and drop in at the Cabaret Las Vegas, a decidedly second-rate but wonderful nightclub, and watch musicians, dancers, rappers, magicians, comics, and crooners take the stage in an all-night variety show. The Las Vegas appears in Pedro Juan Gutiérrez's fiction, *Dirty Havana Trilogy*, but its main literary characters appear in *Three Trapped Tigers*, Guillermo Cabrera Infante's masterful and bawdy 1960s novel set in Havana's early Castro years. The book's narrator, who wears many hats but sometimes little else, hangs out at the Las Vegas, where a wide variety of fleshy entertainers murmur bad puns in his ear. I finally made a point of going inside, where I saw fifteen tables, all within whispering distance of the stage, a slightly raised affair beneath hanging red lightbulbs. A Cuban friend joined me just before the opening act came on. A little cutie hopping tables came by selling in-house lottery tickets for a dollar each; we bought a few and kissed our greenbacks goodbye.

A nine-piece band in similar but not matching gold-flecked outfits took the stage and honked a few practice notes, and suddenly five *muchachas* came out dancing, undulating here, swiveling there, rotating their hips, and rolling their shoulders. Throughout the United States there is this fascination with all things Cuban—their music and dancing, the food they cook, the baseball they play, and the movies they make. Well I'm here to tell you there are lousy Cuban dancers, Havana musicians who can't carry a tune, substandard food, and batters who always ground into double plays. In a way it was refreshing to see this second-rate revue put on by third-tier entertainers.

The muchachas danced in earnest but seldom in synch, their tattered fishnet stockings running before our eyes, their cardboard tiaras slightly askew. We leaned back and smiled; there was so much noise we could do little else. My friend passed out Cohibas, and I lit up my annual *habano*.

I first noticed the Las Vegas when I'd ride an empty bus home from my girlfriend's house at three in the morning. I was punch-drunk in love and lust, and the only street life at that hour between Havana's Chinatown and my apartment in Vedado took place at the Las Vegas. I thought of my friend Jesús, who told me that as a kid he used to curl up to the cabaret's back wall and listen to the music as it wafted out through the exhaust fan. Each time I rode past the place on Infanta, a wide street dividing the Vedado and Centro Habana neighborhoods, I was curious what went on within, but never enough to get off the bus. Attractive abstract ceramic street art identifies the club, which by day is a poorly lighted neighborhood hangout. From ten at night to four in the morning a tattered velvet rope intended to add a touch of glamour keeps patrons in line as they prepare to pay the five-dollar cover charge. Yet as often as I'd passed the cabaret I'd never seen a line. The velvet rope hung alone.

This particular night a solo singer stood on stage crooning ballads. She was nicely turned out in a dark, well-cut calf-length dress and strode across the floor to our table singing only slightly off-key into her cordless mike. Believe me, we would have been better served had she carried a mikeless cord. A couple in their late fifties at the far end of the room spent the time in heavy petting.

On through the evening it went, one ten-minute act after another—dancers, singers, rappers, and musicians hoping to graduate to fancier clubs, or else washed-up entertainers who aspired to nothing more than to be asked back the following night. This was the minor leagues of Cuban cabarets.

A couple of years previous I had met a Havana street magician who pulled rabbits from hats, performed great sleight-of-hand, and fooled me with all the artful deceit his profession demands. "Come see my complete show at the Las Vegas," he implored. "I go on at eleven every night." When I dropped in a few evenings later I learned that the magician himself had disappeared. Too bad, too, because his act at the Las Vegas served as the perfect metaphor for what's been happening since the Soviet Union imploded and Cuba was cut adrift.

A new band took the stage. It sounded like Blood, Sweat & Tears had gone through a time warp and reappeared in Havana. Some of the earlier dancers were back in formation, this time with elaborate falls hanging awkwardly from their own hair.

Antonio Oñate, who lives around the corner, remembers when the Las Vegas opened. With closed eyes and open heart, Oñate spilled out his fond memories of the Las Vegas, his neighborhood cabaret for almost half a century now. An energetic fellow about five-foot-eight with abundant curly gray hair and a mouth full of healthy teeth, Antonio insisted that the "golden age" of the Las Vegas extended from its opening to 1959. In those days the favorite drink there was the Negrona. The place has gone through five-year cycles of being a class act to being a tawdry hangout. By the early 1990s it had become a discotheque, often closed down due to excessive street brawls. Recreotur, the government outfit that eventually ran the Las Vegas, installed Arnulfo Pimienta as its manager, and according to Oñate he's improved the service and the entertainment. "Thanks to Pimienta, the Las Vegas has come back again to become a good cabaret. These days it's a quiet and peaceful place where you can still come and enjoy a nice evening with a group of friends."

One of the best things about the Las Vegas is that you seldom find it in any guidebooks. Although foreigners are welcome—Italians filled the next table—it's a decidedly Cuban hangout. As for the name, the two histories I heard on the street were dead wrong. One—it was named for the tobacco-growing lowlands, *las vegas*. Wrong. Two—it was named in honor of its Nevada counterpart. Wrong again. The original owner back in capitalist days was César Vegas. He named the joint after his family. Vegas long ago left Cuba for Puerto Rico, where he works in a church.

———

Listen closely to what people on the street call *norteamericanos* at the Las Vegas or elsewhere. If it sounds like "yuma," you've got good ears. In Cuban street slang, *yuma* means a foreigner, more specifically, someone from a non-Spanish-speaking European or North American country, and most particularly from the United States. When someone asks my brother-in-law where to find his sister, he might say, "*Se fue pa' la yuma.*" She went to the States. Or an American tourist strolling down Havana's Prado might hear, "*¡Oye, yuma! ¡Ven acá!*" Hey 'merican, com'ere!

Cubans have always liked our westerns, going back deep into the Batista years, and the Glenn Ford classic *3:10 to Yuma* is among the favorites. The movie, popular in theaters and on Cuban television, is quintessentially American. Based on a 1953 Elmore Leonard short story, it portrays the nuances of cowboy honor and obligation. In the quirky way that one language absorbs the sounds and images of another, Cuba, which has embraced so many American totems, has taken *Yuma* if not to its heart, at least to its tongue. The Cuban street-slang *yuma* derives directly from the film.

Late one Havana afternoon, hot on the *yuma* trail, I dropped in on Fernando Carr, a word maven whose language column in the weekly *Bohemia*, "Gazapo," keeps Cubans on the linguistic straight and narrow. It would be tempting to call Carr the Cuban William Safire, but looking north from Havana, I always considered Safire the American Fernando Carr.

Carr lives in an apartment on Salvador Allende Avenue, a street everyone calls by its prior moniker, Carlos III. When I stepped off the elevator on his floor I gave thanks that no power blackout had taken place during the previous forty-five seconds; the Special Period applied to elevators too. I brought along a bottle of rum—de rigueur for a foreigner visiting a Cuban for the first time—and with some ice cubes Carr retrieved from a neighbor's refrigerator we climbed a ladder to his building's rooftop. There we sipped Havana Club as my host pointed out landmarks on the Havana skyline: nearby, the old American-owned telephone company; farther away, the cluster of buildings at the Plaza de la Revolución where Pope John Paul II—himself a *yuma*—celebrated mass in 1998. I pointed waaay off to the north and a little west, and said, "*La yuma, ¿verdad?*" The United States, right? Carr nodded, agreeing that indeed the word likely came from *3:10 to Yuma*. Moreover, he thought it was reinforced by the similarity between the first syllables of *Yew*-ma and *Yew*-nited States. Next time I see Carr I'll present him with "Cubana Be, Cubana Bop," eight syllables that ought to keep the linguist busy for a while.

Carr is a habanero through and through. He echoed the Cuban painter Wifredo Lam, who said, "Cuba is Havana. The rest is mere scenery." As for Oriente-born author Guillermo Cabrera Infante, who spent more than half his life self-exiled in London, "Cuba doesn't interest me whatsoever, but Havana consumes me."

Hence my perennial advice: try to get outside Havana. The people move slower and the air feels more Caribbean. The dollarization of Cuban culture has not yet dominated the countryside, but foreigners have wandered down just about every paved road, slept in farmers' haystacks, and received emergency medical treatment in the most unpopulated regions of the country.

One day near sunset I tried to find a town near the south coast that I'd heard had available lodging. I carefully followed the backcountry roads on a detailed map I carried with me until I arrived at a village at the end of the blacktop. I pulled up to the plaza where an elderly gent wearing a Spanish beret sat by himself. "I thought this road continued through town to the highway," I said, holding up my map.

With his cane he pointed back down the road I'd just come to town on. "You must have that German map," he said with a chuckle. "Every few days someone comes here looking for a road that doesn't exist, and every one of you has that German map."

I looked at the fine print in the corner, and indeed the map was produced in Germany. We lost travelers were the fellow's only source of entertainment, and he invited me to sit a spell and chat.

He was known as El Blanco—Whitey—he said, but there were fewer and fewer villagers left to call him that. The town had no industry, and farm labor opportunities were shrinking. Many of his neighbors had gone to Havana to try their luck. Officials in Havana, alarmed that their overcrowded city was growing yet further, began checking ID cards and sending easterners back home.

To many travelers, Whitey and his neighbors have a certain incorruptible integrity. It stems not from what they have but from what they don't: global consumerism. The U.S. embargo, nasty and reprehensible as it is, has helped isolate Cuban culture from the excesses of our own, and while many Cubans eagerly anticipate the homogenized offerings that may surge into their country in the post-Castro years, it is likewise with a certain sense of foreboding.

━━━

One drizzly night some friends and I abandoned Havana's crowded barrios and tourist hotels for an evening at the Salón Rosado at the Tropicana Brewery and plunked down ten pesos each (about 50 cents) to see Los Van Van, the best dance band north of the South

Pole. Unseasonable weather, poor publicity, and lack of public transportation kept the crowd to two hundred in a space that held ten times
that. Buoyed by some Havana Club, we felt like royalty at a command
performance. Every note came through with remarkable clarity—each
drumbeat, the blare of the horns, the roller coaster of the violins, the
crawling bass line, the syncopated flute, the wide-ranging keyboard,
and of course the street-sly lyrics, sung with a nod and a wink. Los Van
Van play music that fills the spaces between the notes, that compels
the body to move, that dominates octaves, decades, and ideologies.
They play as tightly as their drums, as intoxicating as their native rum.
It is the Caribbean Wall of Sound.

The band, founded by the late bassist Juan Formell in 1969,
quickly took a commanding position in Cuban pop music by tinkering
with the traditional *son* and coming up with *songo*, an innovative style
that overlays rock and jazz, adds instruments new to popular dance
music, and has double entendre lyrics. Some fifteen strong in those
days, the band could be identified as much by its tightly choreographed
movements as by the distinctive appearance of two of its singers, the
dapper Pedro Calvo, a dandy in his wide-brimmed straw hat and
natty double-breasted suits; and Mayito Rivera, who has the moves
of a stage-smart rock-n-roll rapper. "*¡La Habana no aguanta más!*" he
sang of the country's social conditions. Havana can't take it any more!
Another Van Van song popular in the capital's overrun barrios told
of the magical carpenters who manage to create yet more space out
of already cramped living quarters. "*Artesanos del espacio*," it's called,
Artisans of Space. Los Van Van gives sassy voice to those who have
the least.

The full complement plays "salsa with conservatory chops," writes
Latin music expert Enrique Fernández, "barrio music without lumpen
crassness, a fusion of black and white elegance." They know what
they're doing.

Los Van Van was playing Latin America and Europe with
increasing frequency; as a result, catching them at home was hit or

miss. Even when they played dates within Cuba, finding them—or any other group—could be daunting. Back then Havana lacked any reliable, comprehensive entertainment guide, either for Cubans or visitors. Still, some advice: at the corner of Twenty-Third and L in the Vedado neighborhood you can sometimes find a placard announcing the acts at the Salón Rosado. The Teatro Nacional offers a choice of the Piano Bar upstairs, with cool acoustic sounds, or the Cafe Cantante downstairs, which, on last inspection, had watered-down drinks, a second-rate band, and a flood of hookers. Listen for more spontaneous sound at Parque John Lennon at Sixth and Seventeenth Streets in Vedado. Some of the smaller, neighborhood cultural centers have first-rate entertainment—last time out I saw Anacaona, a sexy twelve-woman band with bass guitar, two saxophones, a flute, lots of percussion, and a stunning six-foot trombone player who managed to hit every note while dancing a mean salsa.

Humor, music, and sex were among the few things that couldn't be rationed, even during the Special Period, and an evening with Los Van Van or any of a dozen other Cuban bands will renew any lingering appetite for all three.

———

No slice of Cuban life is less understood by outsiders than its African-based religions—not its athletic prowess nor its government's colossal miscalculations nor the power of a machete during the sugar harvest nor its devotion to José Martí. You could visit here for weeks and not encounter Afro-Cuban religion, go home, and be none the wiser. But it's here, it's in the air, people wear it on their bodies, you can hear it if you listen, you can see it if you want. It's even in my family, and I'm not confident I entirely understand it either.

Until recent decades polite society considered Afro-Cuban religions something to dismiss, practiced only by la chusma—the lowest of the low—tucked away out of sight. Gradually, however, the religions surfaced—their music assertive, their rituals open, their societies and deities accessible to all. Brought to the Caribbean by slaves and practiced under cover of Catholicism, these religions now draw domestic respectability and worldwide attention. The easiest way to catch a comfortable glimpse of them is on a small side street in Cayo Hueso, a working-class barrio of Centro Habana. On Sundays neighbors start gathering on Callejón de Hamel before noon, joined by habaneros from other parts of town and, now, a considerable turnout of visitors from abroad.

Since 1990 Hamel has grown from an unkempt back alley to a site for impressionistic Afro-Cuban art, music, dance, and drumming. Salvador González deserves credit for this, beginning the transition when he was in his forties with a block-long mural overpowering in theme, presence, and execution. Spinning smoke, water, limbs, eyes, and roots surround feathers, goddesses, and serpents. Yemayá and Ochun, both deities of the Yoruba sect, entwine; others from the Abakuá dominate adjoining segments of the mural. The most recent addition is a thematic paint job on the back sides of the run-down five-story apartment houses that line the *callejón*, all the way up to the rooftop water tanks hundreds of feet above street level.

The Jovellanos, a musical group from Matanzas, had already begun when I arrived. They played on the sweltering street, shaded beneath corrugated tin. The group's four drummers could be heard blocks away, and soon the crowd grew to two hundred sweaty onlookers, mesmerized by the full-throttle beat as first the singers chanted Yoruba and other incantations, then danced a wild yet precise ritual whose increasing momentum summoned just the right frenzy. The first number was a soft *yambú* in which a couple acted out in slow motion a rooster and his hen circling and pecking, lunging and leaning. It was meant to be erotic and provocative, and it was both. Next came a faster rumba with rattling maracas that crescendoed as the dancers acted out a fight, then made up as the woman pushed off the man with a turn of the torso, coyly drawing him under her spell. The conga and the *batá* drums were the lead instruments, accompanied by rhythmic clatter from gourds, a cowbell, and well-defined non-Western free-form singing.

Next, the *guaguancó*, sweat-drenched dancers' hips and groins gyrating in sync inches from each other, moving forward, sideways, backward, arms flailing, bodies slowing, building up again, thrusting, almost brushing each other, then pausing, the dancers impressing each other and the captivated crowd.

It was wonderfully suggestive; you can get hot just writing about it.

During a break in the dancing, people strolled the alley reading Salvador's philosophical graffiti, admiring the elaborate structures he's built. He has a storefront art gallery and a regular work crew, and on weekdays he paces the street, remote phone in hand. He's built a crude temple inspired by *palo monte*, a religion with its roots in the Congo and its branches in the New World. It's a lean-to made with sticks from the Zapata swampland on Cuba's south coast, with a lifelike couple seated in front of jungle growth. Salvador stopped to explain his complex composition. "It symbolizes the powerful force of nature," he said, "the waters of the sea, the strength of the rivers, and the volcanic energy we feel from the land. This temple is alive. Look." He reached far back into the altar, pulled out a machete, and hacked out eyes, a nose, and a mouth in what obviously was not volcanic rock at all. It was the outer growth of a tree stump, still very much alive with thousands of termites that erupted as Salvador sculpted his work.

As for the turnout, Alba Rodríguez a, hospital janitor who lives around the corner, said she's been coming to the Sunday rumbas faithfully ever since they began. "I tell people at work to come, but some of them say no, they're not interested in this, they don't like it. For me, it's *tranquilo. Tranquilo.*"

The crowd eventually thinned out, carrying with it the energy of the rumba. On their way out they passed an empty herb stand, then one of the many dictums painted on the wall: *I can wait longer than you, because I am time itself.*

—

We were sitting on a bench in downtown Havana, Manolo and I, chatting about the weather, talking about his health, nodding to pedestrians strolling by. I was on the island to research José Martí, the country's universal hero who, more than a century ago, laid the political and intellectual foundation for its war of independence against Spain. Manolo had paused during his morning constitutional, and that bench was all we had in common. Our conversation was politely interrupted by an officer from the Specialized Police, as they are called, a force made up of somber, cane-thin mulattos from the interior wearing gray berets. He asked for our identification papers, something not uncommon when a light-skinned foreigner is chatting with a dark-skinned Cuban, then walked away after writing down our data. He returned a couple of minutes later. "Follow me," he said, motioning us to his squad car.

This was a miserable way to begin my trip but an excellent way to take Cuba's temperature. He turned us over to a higher-ranking officer who asked if I had any papers with me beyond the few loose sheets stuffed in a small notebook I carried. I had none. Suddenly they put Manolo up against the car, patted him down, handcuffed his hands behind his back, and stuffed him in the backseat. I was not patted down, nor was I cuffed, but they maneuvered me in the other side, and off we drove to the police station.

It was a *Dragnet*-era cop shop, with a high desk and cops milling about. I was bumped higher and higher in officialdom, each officer asking if I had any other papers with me. Finally they ushered me into a large room where a uniformed immigration officer from the Interior Ministry, about fifty, looked up from his computer screen. His office had two very bad paintings of Che Guevara on the wall and a television tuned to Saturday morning cartoons. The fellow was husky, almost chubby, and his conversation was friendly, or at least not hostile. He too asked about any papers. "Why is everyone asking about papers?" He replied with a shrug.

Finally a heavyset plainclothesman from State Security came in, accompanied by three underlings who remained silent. His hair resembled a small, dark yarmulke slightly askew. He likewise inquired about papers, then suddenly thrust a sheet of paper in front of my face. "Have you ever seen this?" he asked sternly. I looked at it carefully. It was the United Nations Human Rights Declaration of 1948. "I've heard of it, yes"—I chose my words carefully —"but this is the first time I've actually seen a copy." "Are you sure?" He paused. "We are not opposed to this document, I want you to understand." I thought of the Seinfeld line, "Not that there's anything wrong with it." "I'm sure I've never seen a copy. But what does this have to do with me?" "How about these?" He dramatically revealed a short stack of the same document. "*No he visto ni siquiera uno entre una docena de estos,*" I said. I've never seen one or a dozen of those. I was unaware of it at the time, but the previous evening police in Havana's Arroyo Naranjo neighborhood were stopping people, inquiring about someone who was tossing antigovernment propaganda from a moving car.

By this time close to a dozen police of all flavors were gathered about me. My interrogator relented slightly. "Someone fitting your description has been handing these out," he said, then repeated his Seinfeldian disclaimer.

"Well, it wasn't me." At that, he nodded, whispered furtively with his cohorts, then left the room.

Fifteen minutes later I was released from custody. The black-market taxi driver I hailed for a ride back to my lodging was named Fidel. "My brother's name is Raúl. Our parents were very revolutionary." I never learned what happened to Manolo.

———

Elizardo Sánchez, a high-profile human rights activist on the island, thinks that the human rights pattern under Raúl Castro has been fewer arrests and jailings and more brief detentions and releases without arrest. "Our day-to-day observation leads us to think that the style of political repression has changed," Sánchez told the international press. Certainly my two-hour incident, singular as it was for State Security and for me, fit this pattern of catch and release.

Raúl Castro had surprised a lot of people. I had last been in Cuba a year earlier, before attitudes and opinions took full shape, and saw a dismal population going about its daily business getting provisions for the following day. That's still what they do for the most part, but this time there is definitely more money in circulation, more low-end street commerce, and a somewhat lessened sense of perpetual anguish. Whoever I talked with in Havana, its suburbs, or out in the provinces, Cubans spoke—if not well, at least respectfully of their temporary president. One, in the privacy of his living room, commented on the younger Castro's lifelong military career. "He knows how to delegate. Things are running smoother." Another, speaking in a restaurant where others could hear, thought Raúl was more understanding of everyday hardships. "He lives in a real neighborhood and understands the street."

Fidel fatigue underlay some of this new attitude. A change—any change—is welcomed, as long as circumstances get no worse. My informal, unscientific survey took me to La Víbora, a once-tidy neighborhood that rarely sees a foreigner. A longtime acquaintance there had once been a well-regarded scientist, but the contradictions of what was said and what was done compelled her to leave government work and find solace in the Catholic Church. She described a devastating rainfall that weeks earlier had pounded the eastern end of the island. People lost their homes, roads were destroyed, buildings collapsed, railroad lines were uprooted. The fragile infrastructure got drenched. "If Fidel had been in charge he'd have started a speech that would still be going, and he'd blame the imperialists for the storm. Raúl devoted three sentences to it in a speech and blamed climatic changes. He told us the ruin came to $499 million and he ordered repair crews to work on the damage." Through her church she makes humanitarian visits to prisons, and she credits Raúl with a measure of expanded inmate rehabilitation programs. "I tell you," she said, "I've known two leaders in my life, Fidel and Raúl. I'm not a fan of Raúl's, but I believe what I see."

Another indicator of Havana's mood took place with a dozen artists, filmmakers, and writers from their early thirties to their mid-fifties sitting around a table of good will, Havana Club rum filling copita after copita. Introductions were made all around, and one fellow laughed at the time years ago when culture authorities tried to eliminate rock and roll because it was considered counter-revolutionary. Everyone lifted their cups at the distant memory, and someone else talked about the difficulty the late Virgilio Piñera, a gay poet with offbeat attitudes, experienced getting published. The table nodded, and someone piped up—"Clothes. Remember we were told we couldn't wear narrow straight pants?" "Yes, and we couldn't wear our hair in Afros! They said it was ideologically disruptive." More laughter. I started to hum Dean Martin's "Memories Are Made of This."

"I got in trouble once for putting Donna Summer's name on my clothes!" a fellow said. "I used to listen to the Beatles on a cassette player in the bushes down by the Almandares." One by one, these intellectuals one-upped each other, chortling at moments of authoritarian rule under Fidel. They spoke of the era of cultural autocracy in the past tense, as if it had happened under a previous regime. I asked if they could have had this conversation twenty years ago. "Are you kidding?" a woman replied. "It would have been suspect just to have a dozen people meeting like this." The liberating air of Fidel's absence gave them enough freedom to indulge in repression nostalgia.

The rhythm of the moment is reggaeton. Under Fidel it was salsa. Reggaeton fills theaters with mad, passionate cheering. At the Teatro América I saw thousands of vibrant Cubans applaud wildly, singing along with the two-man Gente de Zona, whose songs they knew by heart from radio play. For their part, Gente de Zona, suspenders and gold chains drooping at their sides, poured beer on their bare chests to better reflect the spotlight. Raúl and Fidel were far away.

Out in the provinces life went on much as in the past, regardless of who headed the government. In Camagüey, long supportive of Fidel, the streets were as full of bicycles are they were of cars. The bread man pulled his three-wheeled cart through residential neighborhoods selling loaves of soft white bread with a crumbly crust for five pesos— about a quarter—while another street merchant bought empty rum bottles for one peso to sell for a modest profit at a recycling center. A local businessman watching the passing scene with me reflected on his country's perpetual hardships that, despite Raúl, were still glaringly apparent. "What we need," he finally said, "is a Cuban Gorbachev."

THE STREETS OF 1898

To learn the story of the USS *Maine*, pull up a rickety wooden chair at Dos Hermanos, a dockside bar on Avenida del Puerto in Havana's sprawling harbor district. If you had been out with pre-Lenten celebrants at Dos Hermanos on February 15, 1898, you would have seen a shiny American battleship dominating the bay. Cuba, then fighting for its independence from Spain, had drawn the world's attention for the tenacity of its guerrilla forces against a sophisticated European power. Off and on for decades the notion of Cuba Libre, a free Cuba, had motivated the country's intellectuals, campesinos, and slaves. The intermittent war attracted a youthful Winston Churchill, an aging Clara Barton, and a host of other foreigners for a firsthand look at the insurgency and its ghastly consequences.

The harbor was busy in early 1898. Since its arrival three weeks earlier, the *Maine* had been moored to buoy number four between a Spanish ship, the *Alfonso XII*, and a German cruiser, the *Gneisenau*. Earlier that day the *City of Washington*, a Ward Line steamer full of Americans, had arrived and anchored about three hundred yards away. Bars like Dos Hermanos were full of sailors, dockhands, international traders, and the habaneros who catered to them. Spain had recently given a measure of autonomy to Cuba, a move that satisfied neither the liberationists, who demanded full independence; the Spanish merchants, who benefited from colonialism; nor the occupying army, which ceded power reluctantly. General Ramón Blanco, who had been installed by Spain as Cuba's governor-general only three months earlier, had an impossible task. He and his underlings received the *Maine* with politic cordiality. His men gave Captain Charles D. Sigsbee and his officers a case of Spanish sherry, locally rolled cigars, and box seats to the bullfights. At Dos Hermanos and other bars, Spanish wine flowed.

On board the *Maine* that Tuesday night, some sailors danced to an accordion in the starboard gangway; elsewhere another crewman plucked the strings of a mandolin. Shortly after nine o'clock you might have heard C. H. Newton, the *Maine*'s bugler from Washington, D.C., blow "Taps." The ship bobbed listlessly, its nose pointing slightly northwest through the harbor's narrow entrance toward Key West, its imposing one-hundred-plus-yard length visible from stem to stern for all Havana to see. The three-year-old vessel, despite its rank as a "second-class" battleship, was well known within the military establishment. "I wish there was a way that the *Maine* was going to be used against some foreign power," Assistant Secretary of the Navy Theodore Roosevelt had written a month earlier, "by preference Germany, but I'd take even Spain if nothing better offered."

At 9:40 p.m. the *Maine*'s forward end lifted itself from the water. A rumbling explosion echoed along the pier. Within seconds another eruption, this one deafening and massive, splintered the ship, sending metal, wood, anything that wasn't battened down and most that was flying more than two hundred feet into the air. Bursts of flames and belches of smoke filled the night air; water flooded into the lower decks and rapidly rose to the upper ones. Some sailors were thrown violently from the blazing ship and drowned in the harbor. Others, just falling asleep in their hammocks, were pancaked between bulkheads fused together by the sudden, intense heat. Still more drowned in onboard water or suffocated from the overpowering smoke. In all, 260 of the 354 men on board the *Maine* were killed, including bugler Newton; a half dozen more died of their wounds soon after.

"I first noticed a trembling and buckling of the decks," Private William Anthony of Albany later recalled, "and then this prolonged roar." Lieutenant Commander Richard Wainright remembered he felt "a very heavy shock, and heard the noise of objects falling on deck. I was under the impression that we were being fired upon." William Van Syckel, an American who lived in the town of Regla across the bay from Havana, saw "columns of black smoke, and pieces and parts of the ship . . . were aflame." Marine sergeant Michael Mehan was "fired overboard—lifted clear off the gangway." Each survivor had his own horrific tale of inching along oddly angled dark hallways as water quickly rose past his waist, of gases and smoke, of grasping for lifelines tossed by the rapidly assembled rescue crew of the *Alfonso XII*. The wonder is not that 266 died, but that 88 actually survived. "From the waters and from the ship came the heart-rending cries of our men," recollected the *Maine's* chaplain, John Chidwick. "'Help me! Save me!' Immediately I gave them absolution."

From Dos Hermanos you could feel the explosion as the air thickened and lights suddenly went out; people instinctively streamed toward the dock. The blast hit with such force that Havana's power plant was temporarily knocked out. Firemen rushed to the harbor. The foreign press, a chummy and highly competitive bunch, emerged from their lair at the Hotel Inglaterra coffee shop and raced to the waterfront. (Two of them got by harbor guards by claiming to be ship's officers.)

Captain Sigsbee ordered "all hands abandon ship," then stepped into a small launch himself, the last to leave his sinking ship. The dreadful explosion had taken place less than one hour earlier, but the aftermath seemed to hang in time. Sigsbee went straight to the *City of Washington*, where Spanish officials rushed to offer help and express condolences. There he scribbled a telegram to Washington with the most important words of his life: "*Maine* blown up in Havana harbor at nine forty tonight and destroyed. Many wounded and doubtless more killed or drowned. . . . Public opinion should be suspended until further report. . . . Many Spanish officers, including representatives of General Blanco, now with us to express sympathy." The captain tried to sleep on the Ward Line steamer, but moans from injured sailors in a makeshift sickbay and explosions from his own ship's magazines kept him awake most of the night.

The *Maine* was in Havana, officially, on a "mission of friendly courtesy" and, incidentally, to protect American lives and property should the need arise. Yet the visit was neither spontaneous nor altruistic; the United States had been eyeing Cuba for almost a century, much as you might keep a tempting item on your shopping list for when conditions are right. "I candidly confess," wrote Thomas Jefferson in 1809, "that I have ever looked upon Cuba as the most interesting addition that can be made to our system of States." The following year President James Madison warned Great Britain to keep its hands off the island. And in the late 1820s John Quincy Adams had declared that Cuba and Puerto Rico were "natural appendages to the North American continent," and that Cuba had become "an object of transcendent importance to the commercial and political interests of our Union." He likened the island to an apple that could fall from its native tree and "gravitate only towards the North American Union." Annexing Cuba became a running undercurrent throughout the 1800s.

Spain's repressive strategy in 1896–97 under General Valeriano Weyler called for rounding up everyone in Cuba's rural areas and keeping them concentrated in military townships; this way, revolutionists would either be in captivity or without support in the countryside. This brutal policy led to uncontrolled sickness, rampant starvation, and widespread death; Americans learned of these conditions with increasing horror and sympathized squarely with Cuba Libre. Despite Weyler's ruthless approach, however, the persistent Cuban insurgents were close to exhausting the superior Spanish land forces when the *Maine* arrived on its "friendly" mission. "We're here," says a Marine on board the *Maine* in Elmore Leonard's novel *Cuba Libre*, "in case it looks like the Cubans are gonna take over their own country before we get a chance to do it ourselves." Spain's shameful strategy, coupled with America's longtime lust for Cuba, produced ideal conditions for the United States to enter the fray. Our destiny was manifest; John Quincy Adams's apple finally looked ready to fall.

———

The day after the deadly explosion Spanish authorities offered to bury the dead at Havana's Colón Cemetery, a plan Captain Sigsbee and U.S. consul general Fitzhugh Lee readily accepted. Neither logistics nor climate lent themselves to storing or shipping unidentified mutilated corpses. Flowers and wreaths smothered the coffins lying in state at the captain-general's palace in the hours before the solemn cortège with Spanish and American civilian and military personnel made its through the streets of Havana. General Máximo Gómez, who commanded the Cuban revolutionary army, sent condolences. So did Queen Victoria.

The sheer magnitude of the explosion and its aftermath, coupled with Captain Sigsbee's admonition that the public not rush to judgment, created a bubble of suspended opinion back in the States. It was as if the American public, then almost 70 million strong, had been struck dumb by the tragedy. Newspapers initially reported the catastrophe without elaboration, leaving blame and lurid detail for another day. At first President William McKinley and Secretary of the Navy John Long considered the possibility that the ship's destruction was due to an accident. It could well have been an internal problem; explosions from faulty wiring, self-igniting coal, and spontaneous combustion had plagued the Navy for years.

The bubble of suspended judgment burst the next day when William Randolph Hearst's *New York Journal* screamed THE WAR SHIP *MAINE* WAS SPLIT IN TWO BY AN ENEMY'S SECRET INFERNAL MACHINE. The accompanying story included drawings revealing how an explosive device had been planted beneath the *Maine* and how it was detonated from shore. Joseph Pulitzer's *New York World* gave readers a choice—*MAINE EXPLOSION CAUSED BY BOMB OR TORPEDO?*—and immediately sent a tug to Havana "to learn the truth." The *World*, the *Herald*, and the *Journal*, which offered a $50,000 reward for evidence of a mine, were all eager to send their own divers to investigate. Reporters in Havana were on top of the story, and their editors in the States were determined to squeeze every drop of tragedy possible from their coverage.

From Havana's Hotel Inglaterra, Charles Sigsbee, now a captain without portfolio, composed a second message to the Navy brass, this one coded: "*Maine* was probably destroyed by a mine. It may have been done by accident. I surmise that her berth was planted previous to her arrival; perhaps long ago. I can only surmise this."

The United States and Spain immediately established investigatory panels; diplomacy was their first casualty. The harbor and its waters were Spain's, and the Spanish restrained American divers from nosing about; the *Maine's* mangled torso was American, and the United States restricted Spanish efforts to get a good look. No Spaniards testified before the American inquiry, which was headed by Captain William T. Sampson; no American Navy personnel appeared before the Spanish, led by Captain Pedro del Peral.

The United States had not fought a war it could sink its teeth into since the Civil War, and not on foreign soil since the Mexican War in the late 1840s. All the catalysts that bring on war were in place— land to be grabbed, money to be made, diplomatic trump cards to play, wrongs to be righted, influence to be widened, evil to be avenged, and a military ready to mobilize—all these the *Maine's* explosion galvanized. President McKinley—with "no more backbone than a chocolate éclair," wrote Teddy Roosevelt—wanted to wait until the formal inquiry concluded before calling for war against Spain, but he was about the last American with that much patience. The families of sailors killed on the battleship taunted the president to jump into the fracas. Throughout America, eager teenagers asked where they could enlist. Newspapers fed the fever as congressmen were deluged with mail calling for revenge on Spain. According to one historian, Texas governor Culbertson "sent his Rangers to stand guard on the border, to hurl back an invasion launched by 'Spanish sympathizers.'" And Maine governor Llewellyn, fearing attack by Spain, asked for Navy cruisers to defend his jagged 2,500-mile coastline.

Behind the scenes, Spain refused to sell Cuba outright to the United States. Consul General Lee called for eventual annexation, beginning with occupation. What remained of Cuba's American community started packing. A sense of righteousness descended on rattling sabers; Havana could sniff the foul scent of impending war.

The investigations into the explosion took myriad factors into account. Since neither a geyser of water erupted nor hundreds of dead fish floated to the surface immediately after the explosion, it was likely an onboard accident. But to contradict this, the magazines and bunkers were at normal temperature that evening, which meant the explosion probably came from outside. Were bits of a mine found on the shallow, muddy harbor floor? Could divers detect a major hole in the hull? Did other ships feel shock waves? Naval experts from around the world stepped forward to volunteer their own conjectures.

The Sampson investigation results came back within six weeks: the explosion was not accidental; a mine had exploded beneath the *Maine*. "No evidence has been obtainable," the four Navy jurists added, "fixing the responsibility for the destruction of the *Maine* upon any person or persons." Despite this disclaimer, they might as well have proclaimed Spain guilty of mass murder. Meanwhile, McKinley, in office for only a year, and mindful that his Republican majority Congress was up for reelection in less than nine months, asked for $50 million to beef up the military.

Spain's Captain Peral stitched together his country's evidence, convincing but circumstantial, that the *Maine* was destroyed by the proximity of its magazines to its coal bunkers. In other words, an internal explosion.

Reaction to the *Maine*'s destruction took many forms. Americans grieved, opened up their hearts and wallets to *Maine* widows and orphans, sought solace in religion—and indulged in avarice. Even before the investigations were complete, a Johnstown, New York, glove maker suggested breaking up what was left of the *Maine* into mementos. "The wood," he wrote, "could be made into canes." A nationwide chain letter was the brainchild of a Plainfield, New Jersey, real estate agent who suggested everyone in the country contribute a nickel. The Siegel-Cooper department store asked the government for the *Maine*'s scrap to cut into "souvenirs, buttons, scarf pins, watch charms, medallions . . . and many other attractive trinkets"—all income to be turned over to *Maine* widows and orphans. A Great Falls, Montana, lawyer asked his congressman where to send the $444.25 that a local band had raised at a benefit for *Maine* families.

Albert Smith and Jim Blackton, pioneer newsreel producers, concocted a miniature pole with two flags attached: the Spanish at the top and the U.S. flag at the bottom. Wrote Smith: "The camera took in the full length of the flagstaff as Blackton's bare arm reached in front of the underside of the picture, seized the Spanish flag, and ripped it off. Then, pulling on a cord, he raised the Stars and Stripes to the top of the staff . . . the effect on audiences was sensational."

"Remember the *Maine*!," a slogan first given notoriety by the press, became the five most popular syllables in America. It was printed on peppermint lozenges, buttons, and posters; it appeared in Friday night theater and Sunday morning church sermons. Newsstands sold toy *Maine*s made of highly flammable material; one light and *whoosh!* "Shop windows and family sitting rooms," notes historian Margaret Leech in *In the Days of McKinley*, "enshrined pictures and models of the lost battleship." In Havana, the menu at the Plaza de Luz restaurant included "chicken fricassee a là *Maine*."

On April 25, 1898, Congress formally declared war on Spain; by the end of the summer Spain had ceded Cuba after sea battles at the Santiago de Cuba harbor at the other end of the island from Havana and land battles just outside Santiago at El Caney and San Juan Hill. Admiral George Dewey defeated the Spanish navy in the Pacific one morning at Manila Bay. In addition to Cuba and the Philippines, Spain yielded Puerto Rico and Guam, and ceased to be a sea power. The United States had flexed its muscle on land and ocean, its reputation and influence taking root far from home. It was, wrote U.S. ambassador to Great Britain John Hay, "a splendid little war." When Spain surrendered Cuba, it was not to the long-suffering insurgent forces that had held it at bay, it was to the United States, which had been there only a few months; Cuba was just an onlooker. Despite having coordinated its troops with the U.S. campaign, and notwithstanding the contributions it made to American military strategy, Cuba was shunted to the side, the participants in its decades-long independence struggle reduced to observer status.

———

The *Maine* grew as a symbol in American culture, one as easily understood in midwestern cornfields as in the boardrooms of industry. Hundreds of songs were written about the ship and its fate, most of them titled "Remember the *Maine*." Some were vengeful, others sang of a sailor's dying request, still others simply mourned.

> We'll wave our flags, our country's flag
> shall shine o'er waters deep,
> In honor of our nation's cause
> and of the ones who sleep,

one song pronounced. "Oh! Men of the *Maine*, by treachery slain / Whilst guarding the red, white, and blue," lamented another.

The Advisory Committee for Battleship *Maine* Relief Fund, which accepted donations from all 45 of the United States, handled requests from the families of the 266 *Maine* dead. Relatives wrote letters pleading poverty, and the committee sent money, usually fifty dollars each. U.S. consuls overseas often acted as intermediaries for families of the Irish, Norwegian, German, and other nationalities represented on the *Maine*. "All my happiness, all my hopes went down with the *Maine*," a German immigrant mother wrote of her twenty-six-year-old sailor boy from her home on New York's East Eighty-Third Street.

Shortly after the explosion the body of Lieutenant Friend Jenkins, one of the two officers killed, was shipped home to Allegheny, Pennsylvania, where he lay in state at a local post office. With onlookers waving Cuban flags and the Army and National Guard following behind, Jenkins's coffin led a massive procession into Pittsburgh. The casualties who had been buried in Havana, including bugler Newton, were disinterred at the end of 1899 and reburied at Arlington National Cemetery. Pioneer filmmaker Albert Smith shot three minutes of the funeral procession then rented his silent footage to an opera house where an orchestra accompanied the powerful images. The *Maine* and its aftermath had become the first international incident to be exploited in documentary films.

The Navy asked the *Maine*'s survivors to list their lost possessions and estimate their value. One officer asked to be reimbursed for a full dress coat and trousers, three suits, a tuxedo, three dozen white shirts, three dozen towels, twelve pairs of white gloves, two dozen neckties, two pairs of slippers, a diamond collar button, and a dozen bottles of Listerine.

The ship's assistant engineer John R. Morris committed suicide a few years later. His friends claimed he had a guilty secret: defective electrical wiring and not a Spanish mine had caused the explosion. Other theories abounded. A New Yorker wrote that the motive for blowing up the *Maine* was robbery and claimed to know how much money was stolen and where it was buried. Rumors of mines planted by loyal followers of the sacked General Weyler were not uncommon around Cuba; the U.S. consul at Matanzas said he learned of a plot to blow up the *Maine* a couple of days before the explosion.

It was impossible to forget the *Maine*; its carcass lay awash in Havana Harbor, a grisly tourist attraction and a gruesome reminder of the war. Over the years a stream of suggestions flowed into the Navy Department regarding ways to dispose of the ship's remains. A Kansas lawyer wanted it preserved until the Panama Canal was complete, then towed to San Francisco for display there. Another fellow suggested that the *Maine* be beached along the Havana shoreline, where "it will be an interest to tens of thousands of American travelers." Despite efforts to prevent looting of the battleship's carcass, a Havana merchant a few blocks from Dos Hermanos advertised that in his store shoppers could sit in actual chairs from the *Maine*. Shipping magnate John Arbuckle cabled the secretary of war with a blunt proposal: NAME PRICE SELL *MAINE*. In 1903 the Cuban government told the United States that the ship was a menace to navigation and requested that it be removed right away. Frustrated that the United States did nothing, Cuba let out bids for the ship's removal. One Joseph De Wyckoff landed the contract, paying the Cuban treasury a $2,500 good faith deposit. He solicited investors at one dollar a share: "We invite your attention to the financial possibilities of this undertaking, as well as to the patriotic and sentimental features of it." Nothing came of De Wyckoff's grandiose scheme.

The *Maine* assumed the status of exotica. Its identity borrowed from war and foreign shores, from death, patriotism, sacrifice, and valor. The American public, however, like the Cuban government, grew weary of its location. Congress finally got the hint, and in March 1910 authorized the Army Corps of Engineers to dispose of the twisted metal in Havana Harbor. The Corps stayed at the Plaza Hotel and scratched their collective heads over how best to get rid of the ship while maintaining a sense of its residual dignity. Their prescription: build an immense cofferdam around the *Maine*, pump out the water surrounding the ship, and finally dewater the ship itself. Then, raise it from the bottom of the harbor, outfit it so a tug could haul it out into international waters, and let it sink peacefully to the bottom of the sea. It was an unprecedented engineering feat they had in mind, and during the two years between the authorization and its realization a curious sideshow played out back home. The Navy allowed *Maine* survivors and families of deceased crewmen to apply for relics from the *Maine*, which, as workers progressed on the grand plan, amassed considerably. Cities and war veteran groups could likewise petition for newly uncovered *Maine* remains.

The newly constructed elliptical cofferdam consisted of some twenty interlocking cylinders driven deep into the harbor bottom. In mid-1912, after more than half a year, workers began to pump water out of the enclosure. By the time they were done examining the gunk from the ship they had found skeletal remains of seventy-five more of the *Maine* dead. They also discovered Newton's bugle.

Letters came in from across America—heirs, Spanish War veteran groups, municipalities, they all wanted a piece of the *Maine*. A small New York town asked for a six-inch shell. Kansas City, Kansas, wanted "a memento to use in our parks." Sheldon, North Dakota, got a six-inch shell; Yonkers, New York, a pair of binoculars. Watt Cluverius, a *Maine* midshipman who survived the explosion, asked for a service revolver. Lieutenant Carl Jungen wanted a spyglass. The commander in chief of the United Spanish War Veterans asked for a thousand pounds of scrap brass and bronze to melt down into individual plaques. Veterans groups received gavels carved from *Maine* wood. The Navy had to turn down individuals who had no connection, such as the proud schoolgirl who wrote that she was born a few hours before the *Maine* was blown up. "I don't suppose there is many a little girl that was born on such a great day." She asked a favor: "Send me just a little piece of the *Maine* which I will be proud of. If this is convenient for you I will be greatly obliged." At the bottom of her letter, a Navy bureaucrat wrote NO and underlined it. William Sulzer, the New York congressman who chaired the House Foreign Affairs Committee, wrote for a relic; his request was approved.

Press coverage was remarkably tame, considering its original role in making the *Maine* a symbol of Spanish perfidy. The best it could do was FIRST BONES ARE FOUND ON THE *MAINE* in the *Havana Post* in June 1911. When reports filtered north that pencils and rubber bands had been found, Eberhard Faber, the owner of the Brooklyn pencil plant, wrote the secretary of the Navy: "I feel very confident that some of these goods were of my manufacture, and I would esteem it a great favor if I might be enabled to obtain these goods." A Cuban diver found a ring from the Naval Academy's class of 1895 belonging to Darwin Merritt, the *Maine's* engineer, who drowned on board. The diver surreptitiously pocketed it and later at a Havana cafe sold it to an American reporter. The journalist returned it to the family, who gave it to the Naval Academy.

Other *Maine* souvenirs made their way around Havana, and at least one still remains. The celebrated Cuban poet Dulce María Loynaz, from a Cuban family well known in politics and high society, maintained a teacup collection in her dining room. Shortly after her death at age ninety-four in 1997, I visited her Havana home as workers from the Ministry of Culture inventoried her possessions. Among the artifacts was a teacup from the *Maine*. How she got it, no one could explain.

Captain Sigsbee's effects seemed to withstand the years. Corps workers came up with his inkwell, derby hat, typewriter, and a shaving mug. They also located a chamber pot, a pipe, overshoes, a bugle—and handcuffs. Some *Maine* relics ended up at the Naval Academy or at the Navy Yard in Washington. The ship's mainmast is at Arlington National Cemetery perched next to the burial site of 229 *Maine* sailors. Its foremast stands some forty miles away on the waterfront in Annapolis. For this reason Navy people like to say that the *Maine* is the longest ship in the world.

Cubans had been under three flags between the *Maine's* explosion and the Army's effort to levitate it—Spain's, the American, and their own. And U.S. animosity toward Spain? Despite their enmity during

Cuba's War of Independence, writes British historian Hugh Thomas in his history of Cuba, America "felt more drawn to the chivalrous enemy than to their Cuban allies." They let bygones be bygones. The Navy undertook a second inquiry in late 1911, this one headed by Admiral Charles Vreeland. He and the other four men on his team had the enormous benefit of inspecting the damage to the hull, the plates, and the remaining bulkhead firsthand. Even though they had the advantage of a dry autopsy over Sampson's underwater effort, the panel nonetheless concluded, as Sampson had fourteen years earlier, that the explosion was external. Yet Vreeland's findings subsumed and occasionally corrected data and inferences from the earlier board's conclusions.

On March 16, 1912, with the cofferdam opened and the *Maine* cabled to the tugboat *Osceola*, the ship began its final trip. If you had returned to your seat at Dos Hermanos, you would have had a ringside view. At sunrise, a cannon boomed from La Cabaña fortress protecting the harbor. Coffins carrying the remains of the newly found sailors, which had been solemnly carried through town, were loaded on the USS *North Carolina*, in town to carry the bones back to Washington and, along with the *Birmingham*, to escort the *Maine* on its final journey. At 2:30 the seaward procession began. The hulk of the *Maine*, roses covering what remained of its deck, was towed in front of an estimated 80,000 habaneros, past private yachts out to the Gulf of Mexico. Beyond the three-mile limit, the *Osceola* drifted to a halt and a crew boarded the *Maine* briefly to prepare it for burial. Port captain "Dynamite Johnny" O'Brien, who had been a filibuster during the insurrection against Spain, was the last to leave the sinking ship. "Some thought that the *Maine* appeared to struggle against her fate," he wrote later, "but to my mind there was not only no suggestion of a struggle but in no way could she have met a sweeter or more peaceful end. The sea beckoned to her and she went swiftly and gladly to its bosom."

Nine months later the floor of Havana's harbor was smoothed out. It was as if the *Maine* had never arrived.

You would think that the story of the *Maine* would end as the wreck drifted to the bottom of the sea. Although it came to represent the cause for our entry in the Spanish-American War, it has become clear to historians that had the *Maine* not exploded, some other reason would have catapulted us into the struggle for supremacy in Cuba. For some, such as the late Congressman Barrett O'Hara, who died at age eighty-seven in 1969, the battleship was cause for an annual "Remember the *Maine*" speech on the floor of Congress. Himself a participant in the 1898 conflict, he called the Spanish-American combat "the greatest war in all history." For others the *Maine* became the ship that launched a thousand term papers, its symbolic purpose far outstripping its historic role. Cuban governments invariably paid tribute to the *Maine* victims when speaking of American involvement in their war. In early 1925 during the closing months of President Alfredo Zayas's administration, Cuba dedicated a monument to the *Maine* victims. It consisted of two tall marble columns with an American eagle perched on top. At the base was a plaque listing all those who perished. General John J. Pershing, then sixty-five, spoke at the ceremony.

A year and a half later a vicious hurricane blew through Havana with winds of more than one hundred miles an hour. It sank boats in the harbor, killed some four hundred Cubans—and destroyed the *Maine* monument. A new eagle was sculpted, this one more aerodynamic, and a new monument went up. Cuba became a convenient land for foreigners to invest and vacation in, and Americans did plenty of both.

As shipbuilding became more sophisticated and analytical techniques improved, more and more postmortems acknowledged that the *Maine*'s destruction could have been accidentally self-inflicted. One year into Franklin Roosevelt's first administration, in a curious series of communications that involved FDR, his ambassador to Spain, and the U.S. Naval Academy, the United States acknowledged that no proof existed that the Spanish blew up the *Maine*.

In those days Cuba celebrated "*Maine* Day" every February, and the U.S. ambassador would "hold forth at great length," according to a 1941 guidebook, "about the close ties that bind the two republics." Meanwhile, Dos Hermanos held its own as a well-known waterfront bar. Foreigners such as Isadora Duncan and Federico García Lorca visited, and one could always find businessmen, artists, politicians, sailors, and prostitutes drinking downstairs or eating at the rooftop dining room. As for Charles Sigsbee—"the captain" to the public, "Foxy" to his family—he lived to be seventy-eight, believing to the end that a mine blew up his ship. (His descendants, eligible for twelve-pound plaques from melted-down *Maine* bronze, petitioned the Navy for eleven of them to be spread among the current generation of his family.)

That would wrap up the *Maine* story were it not for two men of enormous ego, both bruised by the American military establishment—Cuban president Fidel Castro and Admiral Hyman Rickover of the U.S. Navy. In the closing weeks of the Eisenhower administration, just after the United States broke off relations with Cuba, the Cuban Council of Ministers called for the "imperialist eagle with all its tragic symbolism, vassalage, and exploitation" to be taken down from atop the *Maine* monument. A new inscription would go up, dedicated TO THE VICTIMS OF THE *MAINE*, SACRIFICED FOR VORACIOUS AMERICAN IMPERIALISM IN ITS EFFORTS TO TAKE CONTROL OF CUBA.

The night of May 1, 1961, two weeks after beating back a U.S.-sponsored invasion at the Bay of Pigs, the Castro government sent a crane out to topple the *Maine* monument eagle. But the eagle was a tough old bird and clung tenaciously to its perch. After a night of huffing and puffing, only half of the eagle had fallen. The next day the crane managed to get the rest of the eagle, but not before someone made off with its head. Both halves were displayed at Havana's Museum of the City, in the same building where the original *Maine* dead lay in state prior to their burial. As for the eagle's head, it was mounted on the wall of the snack bar at the U.S. Interests Section—our nonembassy embassy in Havana—for years.

In Washington, Hyman Rickover, assuming the broad authority vested in a Navy admiral, took it upon himself in the 1970s to reinvestigate the *Maine* explosion. He gathered together first-rate historians and engineers, and after exhaustive investigation they established their conclusion: the *Maine*'s death was self-inflicted. The unintentional suicide was likely the result of a coal bunker fire, the Rickover team found, but whatever its cause, it was absolutely clear that an external force—a mine or torpedo—was not responsible. When the 1976 Rickover report was rereleased in 1995, principals in the admiral's original team affirmed their earlier conclusion and added more supporting evidence.

There are still some who maintain that an external blast was to blame. The plausibility of that and other explanations, cobbled together by a fact here, an assumption there, keeps the ultimate truth of how the *Maine* blew up elusive.

Within Cuba today there are two schools of thought about the *Maine*. The first is widespread and almost entirely wrong. Most Cubans will tell you that the *Maine* was sent to Havana solely as a pretext for entering the war, that the vast majority of crewmen were black, hence expendable, and that all the officers were conveniently ashore when the ship exploded. I heard this from writers and building guards and dozens of others I spoke with along Havana's seaside boulevard and elsewhere. It's Cuba's conventional wisdom. The fact is, you could count the number of blacks in the 354-man crew on the knuckles of your thumbs. As for the officers, all were on board, and two died. Cuban ninth-graders use a history book with this passage: "On the pretext of a friendly mission . . . the *Maine* arrived January 25, 1898; but the reality was something else—the presence of the boat formed part of a vast plan of warfare." *Granma International,* a weekly newspaper published by Cuba's Communist Party, has spoken of the *Maine* as "a U.S. warship exploded by the United States . . . in order to create a motive for intervention"; and of "260 sailors, the majority of them black, [who] died while the officers, all white, were safe on shore."

The other, little-circulated but more knowledgeable point of view comes from Commander Gustavo Placer, a retired naval officer who teaches at Cuba's Academy of the Armed Forces. Placer, a military historian in his fifties, joined me for slow, strong coffee at Dos Hermanos, where a clear view of the *Maine*'s position is now denied by an enormous, busy waterfront building.

"Could it have been the Spanish?" Placer asked rhetorically. "I rule that out because no one puts mines in their own port. There were military and cargo ships at anchorage and there was no state of war. There was no advance notice the *Maine* was coming, and you must remember, the United States was not Spain's enemy; Cuba was. It would have been suicidal for Spain to plant a mine beneath the *Maine*. Could it have been Cuban insurgents? Well, why? How? They didn't have the technical ability, and they were busy fighting a war of independence. They wanted military aid from the Americans, yes, but not military intervention. Also, the Spanish navy was all over the place. A mine is the size of a barrel of oil. You simply cannot sneak one into the harbor and plant it under a foreign warship.

"Could the United States have done it? The *Maine* was among the biggest of its fleet. America was already prepared for war; it did not need a pretext. Could someone have hidden a bomb on board without it being discovered or anyone else knowing? That conspiracy is extremely unlikely." Placer was like a prosecutor summing up his case. "No one has ever claimed responsibility or motive, from any side."

"You notice," he emphasized, "that Sampson got promoted to admiral after he released his investigation. He was evidently rewarded for his conclusion. To call an internal accident an external explosion became the pivotal justification for war. The 1911 investigation had to reach a similar conclusion or the rationale for the entire war would have sunk." Placer had read the Rickover report and, not surprisingly, agreed with its conclusions.

The retired commander and I talked about the *Maine* until dock-workers started filing in for lunch. We left Dos Hermanos and walked through Havana's crowded, narrow downtown streets to a shop where I could buy a nautical map of the harbor. I told him about the eagle's head at the U.S. Interests Section and quoted the end of the printed account adjoining the head: "Let us hope that some day this battered head can be again joined with its body and wings in a gesture of friendship." At this Placer broke his military bearing and let out a coarse laugh. "They just don't understand what the eagle represents, do they?"

———

When all the emotional barnacles have been scraped off the *Maine*, you're left with a battleship that was in the first generation of steel vessels fired by coal rather than propelled by wind. Design flaws during this transition brought on a number of accidents, including some involving self-igniting coal.

I screened film footage at the National Archives of the *Maine* going down for the last time and turned the knob to change its speed, then reversed history by making the ship, with its enormous American flag, come back out of the water. Tinkering with the *Maine's* role in history has given it prominence for more than a hundred years. Even now, in the second century following the explosion, controversy has not yet abandoned the ship. After the bodies recovered from the *Maine* were buried in Havana, bones still occasionally floated to the harbor's surface. Those remains, largely unidentified, were buried at Key West, Florida. In 1997, on the eve of the centennial, the Navy decided to sell off the *Maine* plot, complete with the buried bones. A group in Key West protested this decision. Some people just won't let you forget the *Maine*.

THIRD GEAR

Looking at it from a third-floor balcony in downtown Havana after dark, Ricardo's recently purchased, freshly painted four-door 1956 Chevy Bel Air looked just the ticket. My stepsons, who live in the United States, wanted to show off their homeland to their girlfriends, who had accompanied them to Cuba, and Ricardo had offered to drive the four of them and two others to Cienfuegos, 210 miles distant, and Trinidad, 50 miles farther. Ricardo pulled up at noon sharp the next day, four hours late. The first thing the passengers noticed when they opened the trunk was five five-gallon cans of gas sloshing around where a spare tire should have rested. The car had no gas tank; Ricardo had rigged a plastic siphon from a smaller tank under the dashboard. The four doors shared one outside handle, which was dutifully passed from door to door so each could be opened. Still, happy and optimistic, they poured a ceremonial splash of rum on the car's floorboard for good fortune and lurched away.

After a couple of miles, Leonardo nonchalantly asked about oil. "I don't know," Ricardo replied. "I've never put any in." The Chevy peaked at about thirty-five miles an hour. They stopped every five miles to suck gas into the siphon and feed the engine. Famished by late afternoon, they pulled over to a field and cut stalks of sugar cane to chew on. Then the most shredded of the four tires suddenly exploded, and the seven passengers roamed the nearest small town looking for a replacement. The best they could do was a tractor tire they whittled down to size, then, with borrowed equipment, soldered in place.

Back on the road, a side window fell into the lap of a startled Juan Carlos. The car lacked windshield wipers, rear lights, and bumpers, and none of the dashboard dials worked. Ricardo himself lacked a driver's license. (The car did, however, have a fully functioning theft-alarm system.) The clutch pedal fell through what was left of the floorboard. Often they had to push-start the car after stopping. The '56 Chevy belched into Cienfuegos late that evening.

Ricardo's Chevy is one of an estimated 60,000 pre-1960 American cars roaming Cuba. About 150,000 existed at the time of the 1959 revolution, shortly after which the Detroit auto giants and all American manufacturers were forced to stop sending goods to Cuba to conform to the U.S. embargo. Ricardo's car is far more typical than the ones that art directors love to put on the covers of travel brochures and books about Cuba to evoke nostalgia for times past. Movies set in Cuba likewise turn the jalopies into objects of nostalgia by panning lovingly over a wheel-less Chrysler here or a Plymouth stalled in traffic there.

There is a feeling abroad in the land that Cubans love old American cars. Nothing could be further from the truth. Cubans love new American cars, not old ones, but the newest ones that they can get their hands on are more than five decades old.

To own one of these vintages, known as *cacharros*, or less commonly, *batavias*, in Cuba defines who you are, how you spend your time, and how you wish to be known. When your plugs don't spark, when a faulty brake line can't be repaired, when your engine sputters into a coma, when you run into any of Ricardo's difficulties, you fabricate the equipment yourself, share with a friend, buy from a stranger. Or you put your car on blocks until the right part appears the next day, month, or year. But when your motor purrs, when you accelerate effortlessly from second to third gear, when the doors click into place, you momentarily forget your difficulties and glide for blocks with a prideful smile, until you inevitably run into one of Ricardo's multiple problems. Could there be a more appealing metaphor for today's Cuba than cars from yesterday's America?

Cuba nicely exploits the fleeting nostalgia that envelops foreigners when they first visit the island, so much so that a government agency rents spiffy reconditioned old convertibles for visitors to tool around in. Capitalizing on the past is a time-honored enterprise throughout the world, and Cuba is simply taking advantage of its own limited resources. Most resourceful are the shade-tree mechanics who create parts. A 2002 film, *Yank Tanks*, profiles these "doctors," who think nothing of transplanting a Czech engine under a Buick hood or a Russian carburetor within a DeSoto chassis. One fellow fabricates chrome bumpers on his patio; another makes brake shoes in his home workshop. Old American cars in Cuba, cobbled together from their comatose elders, are variations on the old Johnny Cash song "One Piece at a Time."

It is the foreigners who rhapsodize about the cacharros. Two books—*Cuba Classics*, by Christopher P. Baker, and *Che's Chevrolet, Fidel's Oldsmobile*, by Richard Schweid—speak of a love affair between Cubans and old American cars, but what choice have they had? In *Driving Through Cuba*, the Irishman Carlo Gebler uses his search for a 1959 Cadillac Eldorado Brougham as his leitmotif. (He never finds one.)

The rattletraps, according to Cuban-born Cristina García in her sweet paean to the clunkers in *Cars of Cuba*, "positively explode with a riotous sensuality." Among Cubans on the island, the singer Carlos Varela uses the cars as a metaphor for the 1959 revolution in his song "*La Política No Cabe en la Azucarera*" (roughly, Politics don't fit in the sugar bowl), including the lines: "A friend bought a '59 Chevy / He didn't want to replace any parts / And now it won't budge." If the feared post-Castro foreign plunder of native art, antiques, and coastline takes place, surely pre-1960 cars will become part of the booty.

I once saw a functioning 1934 Plymouth on the streets of Sancti Spíritus, a town of about 100,000 in the island's interior, and I know

how that sensation of visiting a living museum of old cars can unex-
pectedly creep up on you. Informally, when Cuba hands sit around and
consider the opportunities that could arise now that the United States
and Cuba have returned to their senses, some fantasize about getting
into construction, maritime industries, or electronics, businesses that
may burst wide open. But after seeing Ricardo's '56 Chevy, I predict a
great future in low-end auto parts. The Pep Boys, Checker Auto Parts,
AutoZone—that's where it's at for Cuba of the future.

THESE THREE KINGS

José Julián Martí had a high forehead, a receding hairline, bushy eyebrows and mustache, deep-set eyes, a gaunt face, and protruding ears. At five and a half feet, he stood thinner than a stalk of cane. Every day he wore a knee-length black frock coat over baggy trousers and a high-collared white shirt with a black tie. The full impact gave his brooding countenance a funereal sobriety.

That this man is their universal hero unites Cubans everywhere, whether in Havana, Miami, Madrid, Mexico, Montreal, or Tierra del Fuego. José Martí, like so many other Cubans, spent a good deal of his life away from his homeland. Twice he was exiled from Havana to Spain for publicly opposing colonial rule, once at age seventeen and then again following his return eight years later. He was arrested for conspiring against Spain, a charge he was guilty of for the rest of his life. In 1880, after traveling through the Americas and Europe, twenty-seven-year-old "Pepe" Martí settled in New York, a city that remained his base until his fateful trip home fifteen years later. It was a journey whose outcome can be seen in a sculpture at the Avenue of the Americas entrance to Central Park the instant a Spanish bullet struck him dead during his only battle in the War of Independence. Poor Pepe.

Since then, through all sorts of leaders—cruel, benevolent, puppet, enlightened, military—Martí has been a constant star in the

Cuban sky. His appeal derives from his revolutionary fervor, his literary output, his sly personality, his sullen composure, and his Pan Americanism. Scholars consider him the first modernist in Latin American poetry, while the breadth of his political acumen casts him as a descendant of Simón Bolívar. He was a humanist and an optimist whose grief-stricken verse often dealt with nature and love, frequently infused with a subtle sensuality. Today, a Cuban statesman, cheerleader, or basher who wants to make a point has only to consult the twenty-eight-volume *Complete Works of José Martí* and pluck out some pearl of wisdom. The point of view makes no difference, for Martí's pieties, while on the highest moral and ethical plane, have become universal. He can be just as righteously quoted by champions of the well-off first-generation exile community as by Fidel Castro, Cuba's former president, stern grandfather, anchorman, and editor-in-chief. ("We rise for our country, but not above her. To rise above her is to rise against her.") More than a century after Martí wrote them, his words are for everybody; they are one-size-fits-all. ("Rights are to be taken, not requested; seized, not begged for.") The motivating force that drove him was not gaining a reputation for his writing or expertise, but rather for a phrase he coined: *Cuba Libre*.

Martí was born on the second floor of a small house near Havana's main railroad station. Today, the house in Habana Vieja has become a museum, and Martí's likeness and name dominate the Cuban shore like the dawn mist. A chalk white bust of Martí sits in just about every schoolroom in the country. In the 1966 black comedy *Death of a Bureaucrat*, the ubiquitous Martí icons become a running joke, starting with a worker who falls into the machine that continuously churns out the busts. It seems that every street corner has a Martí bust, or at least a billboard with a pithy quote from his poetry or prose. The national library is named for him, as are schools in the countryside, work brigades in the cities, health clinics in the *campo*, parks, stadiums, and streets. An enormous Lincoln Memorial–sized Martí stands in Havana's Plaza de la Revolución.

José Martí's writings can be chopped up so many ways—essays on the Americas, love poems, children's stories, politics, reflections on Jews at Chanukah, independence, women, sports, music—that it is not uncommon to see two or more Martí books published monthly, year after year. The phenomenon resembles Best of Pink Floyd albums, which take a finite body of work and by repackaging extend the group's output indefinitely.

I visited the Martí birthplace museum at the depth of the Special Period, then stepped onto Leonor Pores Street to find a passel of kids playing baseball of sorts—they scampered around a small vest-pocket park, tossing a ball and occasionally hitting it, screaming and carrying on. A couple ran up to me, arms outstretched, hands cupped. *"Dame chicles, dame mawnee."* Give me gum, give me money, they cried out breathlessly, their baseball adrenalin still overflowing. "Shush," said the museum staffer who escorted me to the street as she shooed them off. "Go away." She looked back at me with shame that the muchachos were begging. "This is happening more and more." Then she froze at her own words, gathered herself, and bade me goodbye.

She was quite right. Begging, whether kids playing at it or genuinely needy Cubans sadly approaching foreigners, had become visible. Tectonic social shifts were taking place. Here, in mid–Special Period, Che Guevara's New Man would not recognize his country. In the mid-1990s Cubans were demoralized, disillusioned, and saddened by the day-to-day.

I once rode a bus down Insurgentes Sur, Mexico City's major north-south artery, with my wife. We passed Subway Sandwiches, Alphagraphics, Kentucky Fried Chicken, McDonald's, Pizza Hut, Hertz Rent-a-Car, Chevrolet, and a dozen more neon American franchises. "You know," I said, "you bad-mouth Fidel, but five years after he dies this is what Havana's going to look like. You're going to miss the old fart." "You don't understand," she countered. "This is what we want."

Weekday mornings at the José Martí National Library, a disheveled man in his late sixties mutters to himself as he shuffles in, seats himself at a desk, and spreads out folders, documents, and notebooks. He is among the regulars who straggle in to the library's second-floor reading room one by one. "That's the ambassador," a writer at the next table whispers, motioning to the shuffler. "He knew Fidel during the revolution. In the 1960s he was rumored to be in line for a diplomatic post to some African country. No one knows exactly what he does here, but he shows up every day and spreads out his papers. He's been doing it for years. He never was appointed to anything, but ever since everyone has called him the ambassador."

At the Center for the Study of José Martí, an intellectual institution that fills a resplendent old mansion that once belonged to Pepe's son, workers sit at computers, busy entering the words of "the apostle," as he is sometimes called by worshipers, indexing, cross-indexing, listing key words and hot links. I bought their CD-ROM with all twenty-eight volumes of Martí's works on it. Clearly, if Martí lived in the States today he'd win a MacArthur "genius" grant, and Charlie Rose would interview him.

In the midst of Cuba's transformation, I'm always brought back by its eccentricities, its core integrity, its overbearing contradictions, and its gentle foibles. The 1990s were exciting years to be in Cuba, to watch untried approaches applied to an unprecedented system. Cuba was going through its Cambrian explosion, adapting skeletal architecture to a shapeless anatomy.

Most unnerving and rewarding at the same time, block after block, you'd see sidewalks full of household goods, personal libraries, and family wares for sale. I learned of a fellow who, like so many other Cubans desperate for dollars, was selling his family's belongings on the street. In his case he had stacked up all twenty-eight Martí volumes on the sidewalk. I had seen sets for more than three hundred dollars new, and was prepared to pay well for a good used set. "How much does he want for them?" I asked my intermediary.

Word came back: eighteen dollars. "Wait. Per volume or for the whole set?"

The latter. "José Martí's works lie at the heart of every home library in the country. This man is selling his literary patrimony for peanuts. Is he that desperate for dollars?"

When Barack Obama visited Cuba in March 2016, he invoked José Martí's name in public, a well-received literary maneuver. His host, Raúl Castro, then eighty-five, seemed to enjoy Obama's company. The only high holy name not mentioned was his big brother's, who must have been fuming at the warmth the two leaders shared and how it surged like a wave over downtown Havana.

A while back, when Fidel's mere personality influenced goings-on throughout Latin America, the top editor of a multinational publishing house asked if I could get him in to see the comandante with a proposal that his company publish the commander-in-chief's memoirs. I got him as far as the late Pedro Álvarez Tabío, one of Castro's gatekeepers, who listened earnestly as the editor outlined the project. Álvarez replied that he would present the offer to his boss, cautioning that other similar proposals were afloat.

I was reminded of this when, on the very first page of Norberto Fuentes's fictional Fidel autobiography, "Castro" writes that major publishing houses "have stubbornly pursued me for years. . . . I've been courting their offers equally, leading them on."

Consider us led on.

With his fictional autobiography Fuentes scooped heavyweight publishers and Castro himself, deftly mimicking the Cuban leader's voice, obsessions, and outsized ego. His manias and philosophical passions are front and center. His matter-of-fact brutality and grandiose manipulations shine through. Fuentes captured what seem to me Fidel's private thoughts in 572 pages.

Fuentes was either the best or the worst person to fictionalize Castro's life. He claimed to be a devoted fidelista—slavishly loyal would not be putting it too harshly—who felt at ease in Castro circles during the first thirty years of the regime. He was well connected. But the rapid conviction and execution of two high-level officials in 1989 caused Fuentes to turn coat, and after a failed escape and prison time, he was allowed to go into exile—that is to say, move to Miami.

With such a background Fuentes was trusted by few on either side of the straits. Yet by writing this "autobiography," he has likely purged Castro from his system and can now get on with his life. As for this reader, by page 100 I felt I was no longer reading Norberto Fuentes but Fidel Castro himself.

"Castro" describes his brother Raúl as "insecure . . . hits below the belt . . . shadowy," yet avers that "he quickly embraced what was practical and didn't waste his time on cerebral nonsense." Shortly after describing and rationalizing the death by firing squad of some five hundred members of Fulgencio Batista's military—executions that Raúl oversaw—"Castro" writes, "I don't think he'll execute anyone else in the time he has left on this earth. . . . He's too old for that type of thing now."

Looking back on his meeting with Vice President Richard Nixon in Washington shortly after taking power, "Castro" thinks about the U.S. government: "They don't know me. . . . They don't know what I want or what I'm going to do. From now on it will always be this way."

"Castro" dwells heavily on the Bay of Pigs attack, the Missile Crisis, the revolution, and his favorite topic, himself. ("I hold myself in very high esteem.") About the Bay of Pigs invasion: "If Kennedy had authorized the second air strike, there would have been a straight out war," adding that "there's no doubt they would have wiped us out, but at such a high political cost that not even the United States would have been able to face it." And when it dawns on him that Cuba was irrelevant to the resolution of the U.S.-Soviet missile standoff, the comandante angrily recalls: "Look at that battery of phones. All of them silent. Khrushchev hasn't called."

Castro's revolution was sui generis; nothing like it had ever happened before. Despite his dialectical approach to everything from inviting attractive women ("I don't recall anyone ever turning down the invitation") to organizing the Communist Party, much of what's transpired since 1959 has been impromptu. Fidel Castro has been winging it for more than half a century. Yet his Machiavellian philosophy, as laid out by Fuentes, has its own internal logic—instructive, perhaps, for military and intelligence strategists.

"Castro," for example, calls Che Guevara "a little preppy looking for adventure," and adds that his fierce determination "had nothing to do with authentic convictions, stoicism or will. It was asthma." He writes, "The island was too small for the two of us."

Che spent as little time as possible in Cuba. When the island supported both him and Fidel, Che was always the romantic one. He died too early to become a bobblehead, but at Cuba's streetside folk art tables you can always find tchotchkes de Che. There's Che carved from sea coral or Che key rings or a hand-tooled Che on a leather cushion. My favorite: an eight-inch balsa wood box with Popsicle sticks painted so that if you look at it from one side you see Fidel Castro; from the other, Cuba's José Marti; and head on, Guevara.

At a major speech by Castro in March 1960, the photographer Alberto Díaz Gutiérrez, widely known as Korda, was on the grandstand as Guevara, then president of Cuba's national bank, made his way down the front row. "To the camera," Henri Cartier-Bresson wrote in *Life* magazine, "Che's eyes glow; they coax, entice and mesmerize." That's just what Korda must have thought as Guevara suddenly came into his Leica's viewfinder. He saw Guevara's hard and determined visage, his head tilted slightly, the wispy mustache, his eyes burning as he looked just beyond the foreseeable future.

"*Me asustó*," Korda later said. "I was shaken, physically taken aback."

Over the years I've bought a number of Che keepsakes for my personal collection, but one stands out for its value and durability: an original print of the world-famous photograph of Guevara—the one of him with acne blemishes that look more like battle scars. The photographer was Korda, who before the revolution had earned his living snapping fashion and cheesecake shots.

One foggy evening my friend José took me over to Korda's home; I brought along enough Havana Club rum for the three of us plus Korda's young wife. Korda and I both knew I came with one purpose, but there's a protocol to these things. We chatted and sipped, sipped and chatted, and finally came to a pause.

"Well," Korda finally said, "I understand you're interested in looking at some of my work. Let me get my portfolio." He brought out a leather case with scores of impressive prints. I narrowed down the selection to a half dozen. Then to three. Finally I said, pointing, "I suppose I'm most interested in that one. The famous one."

Korda nodded. He went to a back room and emerged with the photograph.

"How much do you think it's worth?" he asked. I genuinely did not know. I'd never before purchased a famous print personally inscribed by the photographer, a picture that has circled the globe and retained both its historical and its symbolic *raison*. Was its worth in Havana the same as its worth in New York or Prague or Milan? Did its value, close to forty years after it was taken, stem from its subject or its notoriety? I didn't want to insult Korda by offering too little, but I didn't want to be taken, either.

"I don't know," I mumbled truthfully. "Fifty dollars? A hundred dollars? I, uh—" Korda cut me off.

"Normally I am paid three hundred dollars for a print. But you are a friend of José's, and that shows you choose your friends well. Second, you have written about Cuba honorably without resorting to slanderous attacks on our character." I nodded. "And finally, you have married a cubana, so you are one of us." He leaned back in his chair. "I will let you have it for one hundred dollars."

For all my adult life, in countries throughout the Americas, I have bought items small and large, cheap and pricey, tacky and worthy, but never have I negotiated a purchase in which friendship, literature, and love played so significant a role. For this I am indebted to Korda, and as he retrieved the print from a back room, I poured us a celebratory round of Havana Club.

Life's not easy when your last name has an -*esque* attached to it. Finca Vigía—Lookout Farm—was Ernest Hemingway's retreat from fans, sycophants, and hangers-on. When he wanted casual contact with other expats, tourists, or sailors, he met them in Havana at the Floridita bar, but the Finca was his castle. Visitors traveled the twelve miles to San Francisco de Paula from town by invitation only, and René Villareal, Hemingway's doorman, valet, general factotum, chief of staff, aide-de-camp, and the model for Mario in *Islands in the Stream*, would clang the huge bell outside the front door when they arrived. Mr. Way, as he was called locally, wrote in the morning, and he preferred typing next to the bed in his bedroom to the opulent library with its enormous desk, custom-made bookshelves, and splendid view of the city far in the distance. Mary, the last of his four wives, gifted him a tower to work in, but he used it more for storage than creative output. The Oak Park, Illinois, native wrote on his feet, using a Royal portable sitting on top of a thick book resting atop a bookshelf.

Mary Hemingway returned to the fifteen-acre estate after her husband's suicide to collect what papers and possessions she could. She had little alternative but to turn Finca Vigía over to the Cuban government. Since then it has been called the Hemingway Museum, the house left pretty much as if the couple went away for a while and never returned. It could be a Banana Republic advertisement.

I was given dispensation to enter the house and went straight to the living room phonograph records: Bix Beiderbecke, Cole Porter, calypso, classical music; five hundred records in all. Almost every room had a bullfight painting by the Spaniard Roberto Domingo. Hemingway's literary interests bulged far and deep if one judges by his nine thousand books: authors Victor Hugo and Waldo Frank, a book on Jackie Robinson, *The Good Soldier Schweik*, a book by his third wife, journalist Martha Gellhorn (who found Finca Vigía in a newspaper ad), Norman Mailer's *The Naked and the Dead*, *The Red Badge of Courage*, the three-volume *London Times* atlas of the world. Yet what strikes the visitor more than Hemingway's enviable personal library are the heads. He enjoyed killing animals for sport, and each room had its heads and horns, stuffed and mounted. I asked the museum administrator how many there were.

She looked at a couple of the guides. Everyone's shoulders shrugged. "I don't know," said one guide. "We've never counted," said another.

I asked if she could come up with a figure.

"You want an exact number?" She was incredulous.

"Yes," I insisted.

"The heads, or the horns, too?"

"All of it. Everything." Hemingway's whole day, from waking up to the dining room to his office and living room—every room—had the handiwork of taxidermists. While the administrator was counting heads I went back to Hemingway's typewriter. I wanted to see once and for all if it was missing the comma key.

The administrator returned moments after I did. "Twenty-three," she said triumphantly. "There are twenty-three mounted heads and horns in all."

The dining room table was set as if company was expected momentarily. Guests would have a slight breeze and a magnificent view. Had they gone to the back bedroom—it's called "the matrimonial bedroom"—they would have seen books about cats, cookbooks, "and other books appropriate for a wife."

Most revealing about Ernest Hemingway's personal life were the scrawls on the wall next to his bathroom scale. It was an almost day-by-day account of his weight. You can see it drop off as he neared the end of his residence at Finca Vigía.

The farm was always an active place, one that played its role in literature and film. In addition to Hemingway's own *Islands in the Stream*, it's featured in *The Veracruz Blues*, in which Papa punches out a sportswriter who wants to become a novelist; in *Papa and Fidel*, a generous fiction of friendship between the two; and in Edmundo Desnoes's 1967 *Inconsolable Memories*, in which semieducated Elena tells her erudite seen-it-all lover that the house resembles the homes of the Americans who ran the sugar mills before the revolution. "The same furniture and the same American smell."

I left near closing and found a common scene outside. Some English-speaking visitors were trying to communicate with the Spanish-speaking staff. I intervened and met a fellow from Alberta, Canada. He had traveled to Cuba to take part in the International Hemingway Colloquium that began that weekend. "There's another one going on now in France," he offered, and we agreed it was high tide for Hemingway buffs.

———

In the mid-1990s when I was in Cuba I would spend a bit of every day walking part of the four-miles-plus Malecón, chatting with its denizens, warding off its hustlers, letting the sea breeze slap my face. These last few afternoons I have fished too. I've used Ernest Hemingway's name as my bait. I was surprised at what I reeled in, sometimes saddened, occasionally amused, and usually impressed.

Certainly Humberto impressed me. He snapped his line out from a reel his father had left him; nice wrist action. At the mention of Hemingway the thirty-four-year-old announced that he had read *The Old Man and the Sea* and proceeded to recite the first few sentences from memory: "*Era un viejo que pescaba solo en una barca en la corriente del Golfo,*" he intoned, as if reciting the Lord's Prayer, "*y llevaba ochenta y cuatro días sin coger un pez."* He felt a tug but pulled in only his lure. "The first time I read that book it was a very intense experience. I practically idolized Hemingway for how he identified with Cuban fishermen. Nothing can take that away from him. I was raised with a healthy admiration for Hemingway. Then I learned that he went to Africa for big game hunting. He would kill defenseless animals for sport. He was like the sun. He gave us a lot of light, but he had his dark shadows, too."

Now that the sun had gone down more people drifted over to the Malecón, first neighbors from nearby mid-rise tenements, then habaneros from farther inland. Two university students folded up their chess game and walked over to El Rápido, a misnamed hot dog stand. Street talk centered on the bones of Che Guevara, newly uncovered in Bolivia. Everyone was anxious to learn how the government would best exploit this new development. Ernest Hemingway had been in the news, on the radio, and on the streets as well. An international symposium on Hemingway would get under way in a few days. A French crew had just arrived to film a documentary on Hemingway's life, and a Hemingway film festival was under way at the Cine Charlie Chaplin. And Gregorio Fuentes, the captain of Hemingway's fishing boat, celebrated his one-hundredth birthday this week with a round of parties.

"People fish for necessity now," Humberto went on. "In my father's time it was sport fishing. Before the revolution the monthly salary of a doctor could buy a whole marlin. Today a doctor makes so little he couldn't buy five kilos of fish even if he could find it at market. I've read that in the tournaments years ago they used to catch up to sixty marlin in three days. Now they're lucky to pull in a half dozen. The seas around here are almost fished out."

Alejandro, a veterinarian, and Francisco, a mechanic, both unemployed, each had a word about Hemingway. "Cockfights," said the vet. "He loved cockfights." "Prostitutes," said the mechanic. "He had a reputation." They talked about the Marina Hemingway yacht club complex west of town. "It's a good place," Alejandro acknowledged, "but it doesn't affect us. We don't receive any benefit from it. None of the money ever reaches us. Same with The Old Man and the Sea Hotel." They were more interested in American boxer Mike Tyson. Finally Francisco asked how much I would pay for a book by Hemingway in the United States. Five dollars, I said, thinking of used bookstores. "I couldn't afford it," Alejandro said unhappily. He pointed to El Rápido. "Will you buy me a hot dog?" I demurred. "I'm not asking for money." His voice went from friendly to slightly menacing. "I want a hot dog." He shot me a look of disgust, hopped off the seawall, and walked away with his buddy. A minute later a late model rent-a-car sped by, its foreign driver in wrap-around sunglasses, a cell phone grown from his ear. Alejandro and Francisco's sullen attitude was most understandable.

José Antonio, an out-of-work stevedore, had been on the Malecón since eleven at night when I found him there the next morning just before sunrise. Light from Morro Castle—the same lighthouse that welcomed the battleship *Maine* more than a century earlier—still blinked to all the ships at sea. Clouds slept on the Gulf Stream. A lone boat floated by, a solo cyclist pedaled on. José Antonio's weapons were his fishing spool of nylon twine and a guitar that a Canadian tourist gave him three years earlier. Between songs through the night he had caught some half dozen fish, each about four inches long. "With what my wife makes teaching nursery school and the ration book, well, this should be enough to keep my family eating today. I made four dollars singing for tourists last night."

Hemingway interested him only slightly. "He had a fondness for marlin." He started to sing a *guajira* called "El Amor de Mi Bohio." "He became one of the people," he said between verses. "He had a presence here." He put down his guitar.

"You have seen me fish for my family so they can eat, but I haven't been able to buy new clothes in a long time. I was noticing that we wear the same size, so I was wondering—"

I fished in my wallet for a dollar as he stood up straight. The sun also rose.

———

Fernando Campoamor was a bartender and close acquaintance of Ernest Hemingway's. He considered his role as a contemporary of Hemingway's a mixed blessing. Over the years he had seen Hemingway's legacy in Cuba evolve from an acceptably eccentric expatriate to a shamelessly exploited commodity in the marketplace of tourism. Few people called on Campoamor in his last years, and when they did, it was often to solicit help promoting tourist destinations, not to have him reflect on the author who often parked his Chrysler out front and dropped in for a drink. "It's to be expected," he said philosophically when I came by for a drink. "It doesn't bother me." As his friendship with the Nobel Prize winner blossomed, Campoamor gained a reputation as a barman, a fellow who could mix a drink, a stand-up guy who could hold his own.

"The trouble is, my refrigerator has no ice. It's been broken for a month now." Campoamor extended this apology when I asked for my rum on the rocks. A widower since his wife died of complications from Parkinson's a few years earlier, he lived alone in a poorly lighted Vedado apartment full of memories, books, and rickety chairs. Everyone else in his family—siblings and children—had moved overseas.

Campoamor's home had the air of a hospice between residents. He livened up by unscrewing the top off a bottle of añejo. His partially buttoned shirt askew, his glasses cockeyed, his dirty shorts resting at an angle on his hips, he raised his glass. "To the high life!" he toasted. After a sip he rested his shot glass on the table next to his pipe.

"Things are difficult in this country. No one else here smokes a pipe and we have no pipe cleaners." He lamented this omission from the Cuban landscape as if a supply of pipe cleaners would complete his simple life and resolve his country's dilemmas. "I get my tobacco," he said with an impish grin, "from Winston Churchill's personal cigar roller."

We spoke of Cuba's lamentable condition, literature from Brazil, and the fertile red soil in his hometown of Artemisa. "I always defend Cuba," he volunteered. "It's still anti-imperialist, and that's the important thing." How, I asked, will you celebrate the coming centenary of Cuba's independence? "Maybe," he replied, "in the cemetery at Artemisa."

Gregorio Fuentes, the captain of Papa's fishing boat, the *Pilar*, became a tourist attraction in his own right. He and the writer met casually in 1928 when Hemingway was twenty-nine years old and Fuentes a year older. Ten years later they bumped into each other again, and from that moment on Fuentes served Papa as his captain, onboard cook, bartender, fishing adviser, and confidant. "We spent so much time together," Fuentes once told Jacques Cousteau, "he told me I was Hemingway and he was Gregorio."

By all accounts the warmth between Ernest Hemingway, a talented writer, and Gregorio Fuentes, a talented seaman, grew from genuine respect and dewy-eyed affection. The author willed the *Pilar* to his captain. Hemingway referred to Gregorio in a diminutive form: Gregorín. Fuentes called Hemingway Papa, a nickname used only by those close to him and writers who never met him.

Fuentes stood close to six feet tall with a weather-beaten face distorted further by a bulbous nose. He wore a long-sleeved blue shirt tucked into gray slacks. His loafers had tassels. He lunched regularly at La Terraza, courtesy of Cuba's tourism industry. Visitors from all over the world hesitantly approached him. "Are you the old man who went to sea?" they'd ask as he dined on fish soup and shrimp enchilados. His grandson Rafael Valdes handed out business cards reading "GRANDSON AND REPRESENTATIVE OF SR. GREGORIO FUENTES." He arranged interviews with journalists and Hemingway buffs charging from ten to a hundred dollars per session. From the looks of things, Hemingway nostalgia was booming.

Business was also good for Rumbos, the Cuban tourist outfit that oversees La Terraza. Fuentes arrived for his hundredth birthday party in a cap that said CAPITAN, but within minutes the portly president of Rumbos replaced it with one reading RUMBOS. In fact, the birthday party, held in La Terraza's main dining room plastered with photographs of Hemingway, was sponsored by Rumbos. Most of the guests were flacks and public relations functionaries from government agencies, joint venture tourism companies, and pit stops on the Hemingway trail. Fuentes's birthday cake was topped by one candle. As television cameras captured the moment and publicists applauded, Fuentes blew out the flame. No one mentioned that Cojímar was a major departure point for rafters leaving their homeland hoping to reach Florida. At the other end of the cove that La Terraza looks out upon, workers were closing up the Ernest Hemingway Sport Fishing Center. Nearby, a half-mile path of increasingly thick overgrowth opened onto a small beach where vacationing kids splashed in the water. If you looked into the Caribbean, you could easily imagine a hopeful Santiago rowing his lonely skiff out to the Gulf Stream.

In the late 1990s an online travel/adventure magazine called *Mungo Park* sent me to Cuba to prepare for a series of reports under the general heading "Hemingway in Havana." Now defunct, *Mungo Park*—named for an eighteenth- and nineteenth-century Scottish explorer—was owned by Microsoft and operated out of corporate headquarters on the campus in Redmond, Washington. The series of dispatches I was to post daily would conclude with reports from Mariel Hemingway, the actress who was born some twenty weeks after her grandfather's suicide. She was to be flown in for the occasion along with her husband, Steve Crisman, who was shooting footage of her for a documentary film.

I made as many logistics arrangements as I could, given Cuba's perennial suspicion of foreign electronic media. The country was just then emerging from the effects of the Soviet Union's implosion.

Microsoft's reputation helped enormously as I made housing and travel plans and detailed a wide range of destinations on Cuba's informally named "Hemingway Trail." "Will Bill Gates be coming?" officials in the tourism and communications fields invariably asked. "You never know," I replied with a wink.

My most daunting task was to convince Cuba's Catholic Church to take Ernest Hemingway's 1954 Nobel medallion out of hiding so Mariel could see it. The previous year Winston Churchill won the literature Nobel for his histories and biographies. When Ernest received the twenty-three-karat gold medal awarded for *The Old Man and the Sea*, he wanted to give it to the people of Cuba, off whose north coast his book is set. He turned it over to his friend Fernando Campoamor to place in the custody of the Catholic Church for display at the sanctuary at El Cobre, a small town outside Santiago de Cuba on the island's southeast coast. The sanctuary has been called the Cuban Lourdes and remains a repository for mementos and prayers from the hopeful and hopeless. The medallion remained on display for decades until the mid-1980s when thieves broke into the glass display case and stole it. Cuban police recovered the medal within days, but the Catholic Church decided to keep it in hiding rather than chance another theft. So it was with singular pleasure that I negotiated with Padre Jorge Palma of the Diocese of Santiago de Cuba. After a private meeting in his office, at which the padre displayed wicked humor about the pending visit of Pope John Paul II, the Church agreed.

When it came time for the actual online series to begin, *Mungo Park* flew down a photographer whose digital work was to be posted alongside my articles and a producer to oversee the massive engineering and technical details as well as the budget. The day we were to go online the Cuban tourism flack assigned to us had unfortunate news: we had not yet received official permission to begin transmission. CUBATUR was on our side, but State Security—which we later learned had a hotel room on the floor below ours—tried to sabotage us. Producer Christian Kallen took a deep breath and went to work.

Instead of using a direct phone line to the States, which the Cubans monitored, he routed a line from his laptop to a Microsoft terminal in Canada, where the stories and photos were dutifully forwarded to headquarters for online posting the next morning. Every day the tourism fellow sadly told us we had not yet received clearance to transmit, and we'd nod our sad acquiescence. And every night we'd mojo the package to Canada.

Finally, Mariel arrived with her husband plus two factotums who seemed to have no function other than to swap tales about how to extract cash from errant ATM machines. I was only too pleased to guide Ms. Hemingway and her entourage around Havana and introduce her to people and places of note, especially locations associated with her father's father. Each time we came to a site connected to her grandfather I would tell her the conventional wisdom, then explain that the popular story was at odds with the actual historical record. For example, a welcoming sign at a famous restaurant, supposedly autographed by Ernest Hemingway, was a complete forgery invented by tourism officials after his death. A hotel where he lived was said to be where he wrote *For Whom the Bell Tolls*. Actually he wrote most of it at another hotel where he maintained a room to escape his growing popularity. Gregorio Fuentes, Ernest Hemingway's old sea captain, then one hundred years old, was trotted out and heralded as the star of *The Old Man and the Sea*. Actually, as a letter from Hemingway to his editor Max Perkins at Scribners reveals, the real fisherman, initially at least, was someone else who happened to die early on, leaving the way open for a new public face for the novella's protagonist. Mariel's husband grew increasingly annoyed at me puncturing holes in the grand myth he had come to film, and at one point leaned over from the backseat of our rented SUV. "Miller," he said with irritation, "shut up."

We chartered a plane to fly cross-country to Santiago de Cuba, where a driver and van met us at the airport. When we arrived at the church at nearby El Cobre, Padre Jorge Palma came to the chapel to greet us. I'd like to say he unlocked a creaking mahogany box and slowly unwrapped a fringed silk tallit to produce the medallion. But no, Ernest Hemingway's celebrated Nobel Prize, which weighed almost half a pound, was stored in a large manila envelope inside a desk drawer.

Mariel faced the altar and knelt briefly and crossed herself, then rose and received the medallion as the rest of the party watched from a distance. As interpreter, I stood a few discreet feet back and to the side in case my services were needed. Mariel fondled the precious medal, absorbed its essence, then, like a quarterback handing off to his half-back, suddenly turned 120 degrees to her left and placed her grandfather's medallion in my hands.

After many books and decades of writing, I had received the highest honor in my profession, the Nobel Prize for Literature.

I do not know what followed. It seemed as if a ray of sunlight had come through stained glass and struck me dumb. There was something heavy in my hands that reflected the sun, I know, but I'm not sure if I held it for five seconds or five minutes. I recall sweating profusely and wearing a goofy grin. Mariel's voice brought me out of the fog: "OK Tom, that's enough," and I handed the 1954 Nobel Prize for Literature back to her.

On our last day in Cuba the tourism flack, utterly clueless about the previous week's daily Internet postings, excitedly told us we would be allowed to transmit to Redmond that evening. To make him happy we reprogrammed the laptop and did it his way.

LAS PARRANDAS

Eighty-three-year-old Francisca and her fifty-five-year-old daughter Modesta farm and get by, barely. The modest patch of land they jointly plant with beans and other crops lies just downhill from the town of Viñas in Cuba's central province of Villa Clara. Bordering the north coast and covering more than 3,000 square miles, the province has a population of close to 850,000 people, mostly of mixed Spanish and African descent. Except for slight hills that rise inland to the southeast, the province consists of fertile flatlands ideal for sugarcane and cattle grazing. An appliance factory produces pots and pans, while a university in the provincial capital, Santa Clara, draws high-school graduates from the surrounding territory.

From inside her wooden shack, Francisca can see truckloads of cane passing by, a reminder that despite Cuba's unique political identity, the country shares its economic history with the rest of the Caribbean. Back in the mid-1990s, Villa Clara's annual yield was more than a half million tons of sugarcane, about 10 percent of the national crop. Even when tourism became the top money-earner, the sugarcane harvest determined economic prospects during the Special Period.

A frayed electric wire with an empty socket hangs from the ceiling. "There are few lightbulbs in the countryside," Francisca explains. Her sewing machine is host to spiderwebs. "To fix it, I need a part that costs twenty pesos [almost one dollar]. I offered the repairman a trade for beans, but he refused." (The CUC, or convertible peso, was still a few years away.)

The U.S. dollar has become the currency of necessity. Cubans get dollars by working in the tourist industry or for a multinational company, through petty crime, by begging, by playing the black market, or from families overseas. Francisca, a typical *campesina*, is no criminal or beggar; she has no access to the black market and no family abroad to send money for clothing. Her meager crop is her currency. "What can I say? I've always been poor. I went through sixth grade. My husband was a vaquero. He worked on horseback at a nearby farm. He died last year; he was sitting right there." Francisca indicates a wobbly wooden chair next to the handmade table.

We walk a short distance up the road to Modesta's home (a second daughter lives in Havana). The younger woman is spreading beans to dry on her front porch. She divorced her husband because he would come home drunk and beat her. Modesta's four children live nearby, and she sees her six grandchildren frequently. Her material comfort exceeds her mother's. Her handsome two-bedroom home has a twenty-three-inch television, a stereo, and a washing machine. It is filled with furniture made by a carpenter son. "I paid for the house with a loan from the state," she says. I admire a thin quilt covering one bed; the design of white and red crosses interspersed with touches of blue somewhat resembles an Amish motif. "Oh, that? When I have free time and extra cloth, I work on it."

Modesta's kitchen has a two-burner gas stove, but gas has become an almost unobtainable luxury. To prepare a cup of coffee she takes me behind the house to her "rustic kitchen"—an open-air, thatched-roof affair equipped with a woodstove. She fires up some kindling, sets a pot of water to boil, and grinds some homegrown coffee beans. "It's true we have no gas," she remarks, "but we do have a monthly allotment of water. I get firewood with the help of an old man who lives in town; we take his cart into the nearby hills to collect it." This occasional hunt for scrap wood is the most that the mother and daughter do to breach the law. "Here, have a cup of country coffee." I compliment Modesta on her coffee and resourcefulness. "We have to be inventive to live," she says with a laugh. "We're Cubans."

My visit, in December 1996, comes at a good time to take the pulse of Villa Clara, and by extension, the nation as a whole. This is the month that residents busily repair damage incurred during the autumn hurricane season. The small, early harvest to provide sugar for domestic consumption—a sort of spring training before the real season starts for exportable sugar—has just ended, and the big harvest is just getting under way. And December marks the season of *las parrandas*, the raucous fiestas that have been celebrated in some Villa Clara towns for more than a century.

The anniversary of the final, decisive battle of the 1956–59 revolution took place in December, when rebel troops under Che Guevara derailed an armored train filled with government soldiers and won a pitched battle in Santa Clara. The loss was a determining factor in General Fulgencio Batista's decision to flee the country. Bullet holes from that firefight still pockmark the upper façade of Santa Clara's main hotel, where I am staying. (Guevara was killed in 1967 while trying to foment a revolution in Bolivia. In October 1997 his remains were returned to Cuba and entombed in the base of an immense statue of him near the center of Santa Clara.)

Francisca and Modesta's half-acre plot, about eighteen miles southeast of Santa Clara, is still recovering from the onslaught of Hurricane Lili, which invaded Cuba's mainland two months earlier. "Malanga, beans, yuca, avocado, plantains, papaya, everything we had, blown to smithereens," says Modesta. "The television weatherman told us that Lili was gone, but it was right here that whole weekend. We felt it, we lived it! Fortunately, we didn't lose a lot." Lili had advanced along a shifting, unpredictable course. Havana and the west got brutal, sustained rains that severely damaged housing already weak from disrepair, forcing the temporary evacuation of 60,000 inhabitants. Lili stirred up nasty weather throughout the country's midsection too, displacing some 190,000 more. The damage to sugar mills threatened to further depress the already sluggish economy.

One of the pueblos in Lili's path was Calimete, a small sugar town in the province of Matanzas. The hurricane submerged cane roots for days. "The hurricane created a fracas much as General Maceo did!" said Calimete schoolteacher Alicia Albarrán. The story goes that it was here, during the protracted struggle for independence from Spain, that General Antonio Maceo lulled Spanish troops by leaving in one direction only to surprise them by returning from another. Maceo, "the Bronze Titan," proved the master military strategist until his death in battle in 1896.

Lili dropped nearly thirteen inches of rain on Villa Clara, damaging the dwellings of most residents. People who had nowhere to go were stashed in any building that had space and a roof.

In Dolores, a rural community a few miles inland from Caibarién, a vacant school dormitory was pressed into service as an emergency shelter for two dozen people. Many of them had already been directly dependent on the state due to previous personal calamities. Upon my arrival, half of them rush up to tell me their tales of woe. "I've lived on the streets since my mother died," says a barefoot mother who claims to be nineteen but looks five years younger. "I have no family to turn to." She hoists up Antonio, her young son. His body is spotted with dark rashes and his scrotum is grossly enlarged. Another woman, holding her daughter's hand, says, "We've been living in the streets under portals. My daughter is eight, but she's not in school. Where would she go?" A small boy wanders over to the gathering, and the woman whispers loudly, "He's only four, but they've already detected mental disabilities caused by neglect."

They each want to describe their pre-Lili circumstances. An unshaven man approaches, hand outstretched. "I'm Sebastian. I've been living under corrugated tin near the airport." A woman who has recently undergone kidney surgery says, "I lived in one room made of palm fronds." A relatively hefty man joins us: "My shed was metal and wood. I fished for a living, but the hurricane blew away my home. Now I'm trimming growth by the highway." The first woman, the one who looks so young, turns to me. "They should have put us up at Guanajay," she mutters, referring to a notorious prison near Havana. "That would be better than this."

Just as they offer to show me their dormitory, the local political chief arrives and asks what's going on. He forbids the residents to speak with me. I tell him I am not looking for scandal or misery, only a glimpse of how one Caribbean country deals with devastation when a ruinous storm blew through. This does not impress him, and he insists I see the State Security functionary in Caibarién. After a couple of hours and a few phone calls, the Caibarién official says I can continue my work. On my return I am confronted by another local political figure, but this time I am accompanied by a doctor who explains that State Security has approved my visit. "He has written about Cuba in a friendly way. He's against the blockade." Evidently this is the litmus test for a foreign scribe. The administrator does an about-face and leads me into the dormitory. When substantial change visits Cuba's political system, some will adapt with relative ease while others will find it difficult to adjust. The doctor, I reflect, will effortlessly fit into the former category; the local politico into the latter.

The dormitory apparently served as a barracks for migrant laborers during the cane-cutting season, when school was not in session. The living quarters are dirty but livable, with jalousie windows, a tile floor, corrugated-tin roof, and double-decker bunks. The sets of bunks have been haphazardly partitioned off with cardboard dividers, allowing couples and families some minimal privacy. The torn and stained mattresses aren't much thicker than the cardboard frames and wooden crossbars they rest on, and the sheets—the few that there are—are filthy. Although the windows allow in a breeze, a slight stench permeates the place, largely a residue of cooking odors. Most of the showers at the end of the hall are out of service. "We serve them *viandas* [a mix of tubers], rice, potage, and *arroz con leche*," says the official. "We make sure the kids get chocolate milk every day and the adults a soft drink. When there's no milk, we serve sugar water. Some work in the potato fields near here, but when school gets back in session we'll have to find new lodging for all of them. We try to take care of them the best we can. A doctor visits every so often. That boy you saw? We had surgery performed on his scrotum a couple of weeks ago."

The doctor who accompanies me, a helpful fellow in his forties named Miguel Martín, comments that a boy with a rash on his arm has parasites—worms and insects. "These people's problems are compounded by extremely old mattresses in awfully close sleeping quarters without adequate ventilation."

Dr. Martín—known to everyone as Mickey—is an obstetrician-gynecologist who rides the circuit in rural Villa Clara from his base in Remedios, a nicely preserved colonial village. He has written several small books about preventive health care, some for children, and he takes great professional pride in Villa Clara's infant mortality rate—only 5.9 per thousand births, among the lowest in the country, which is also among the lowest in the Americas. Family planning and prenatal care remain high priorities despite the dearth of supplies and medicines in the Special Period. Advertisements promoting condom use are broadcast on television and radio, contraceptives are available, and abortion is common.

In Palacio, a nearby pueblo whose economy depends on sugar processing, I meet Juan Bermúdez, whose neighbors are helping rebuild a home wrecked by Lili. Bermúdez, fifty-eight years old, is convinced he was saved from sure death by a miracle. He was seated at the entrance to his home preparing some food when the hurricane struck with full force. The roof of palm fronds caved in on the stove, erupted into flames, and a supporting beam came crashing down, narrowly missing him. Bermúdez reached out for his gesso image of La Virgen de la Caridad del Cobre, Cuba's patron saint. Then another major gust arrived, only this one carried a torrential rainstorm, dousing the flames. Bermúdez emerged from his house unscathed, clutching the gesso image. He credits the saint with preserving his life. I suspect Juan Bermúdez will be among the faithful when John Paul II visits this province two years hence. The Pope will find that the number of Cubans openly identifying themselves as Catholics has grown since 1991, when the Communist Party allowed religions a higher profile. The latest statistics reveal that 15 percent of Cubans consider themselves atheists while an equal number identify with one specific religion. A clear majority, however, dines at a spiritual smorgasbord of beliefs. Among them are many who call themselves Catholic but who identify equally with Santería, a religion that blends Catholicism with the worship of deities brought by slaves from Africa.

The Special Period dampened but did not drown Cuba's essential frivolities. During the course of a weekend on Santa Clara's main square, one could learn about homemade wine from the Viniculture Club or about growing plants from the Bonsai Cultivation Society. Residents could dance at a late-night disco or watch the National Ballet of Cuba perform *Cinderella*. In the countryside, people passed their spare time playing dominoes, repairing cars, even staging cockfights (betting is banned, fighting roosters are not). And in December, much of eastern Villa Clara prepares for the annual *parrandas*.

The *parrandas* emerged in Remedios in the 1800s from a mixture of year-end religious celebrations, community revelry, uncontrolled pyrotechnics, and—through the quirkiness of late nineteenth-century immigration—Eastern European music. The festivities quickly spread to many other small towns. A pueblo divides itself roughly in half, each side with a geographic or historical identity. Each half builds a float, often sixty feet high, to be hauled to the central plaza. (In small towns with very narrow streets, such as Remedios, they build monstrous stationary displays instead of tractor-pulled floats.) The floats may reflect pop culture (Snow White, outer-space fantasy), international icons (Simón Bolívar, George Washington), or national themes (Cuban tobacco, the successful literacy program). In the center of town the two groups face off in an evening of dancing, drinking, and public-spirited indulgence.

I opt for the *parrandas* in Caibarién because it's on the coast and its neighborhoods are clearly defined—and divided—by allegiance to crops and fish, land and sea. On the appointed night, the two rival floats—laden with blinking lights and waving, costumed residents—lead neighborhood parades through streets lined with stands selling food, knickknacks, and handicraft items of leather and wood. As I wander through the easygoing chaos, it seems like a lively county fair gone slightly haywire. Fireworks cap the evening of cherry bombs.

The *parrandas* draw enthusiastic participation because they are apolitical, determinedly free from the economic burdens that weigh down the other 364 days of the year. The celebration is a link between the villagers and their ancestors, something they proudly hand down to the next generation. The neighborhood rivalries peak before midnight when the floats confront each other; by dawn most celebrants have forgotten which part of town they come from.

UNDUE ROMANTIC PERSUASION

Fidel Castro is dead. He died in his bed in Havana, a city where he wasn't very popular. His cremated ashes were interred in a rock at a cemetery in Santiago de Cuba, where he was very popular. Hundreds of thousands of his countrymen took the time to stand in silent respect as his ashes were carried through the countryside along the reverse route he took in his 1959 revolutionary victory. His revolution lasted from 1959 to 2016.

Those who despised him in life stood erect unprompted. Those who followed Fidel shed silent tears. Quiet schoolchildren line up daily to pay their respects at the Santa Ifigenia cemetery. Goose-stepping uniformed guards change positions every half hour.

Here's a question for all of them, the farmers, truck drivers, black marketeers, students, electricians, and the unemployed: Is Cuba better off now than it was fifty-seven years ago?

━━━

Cuba's proximity and its warmth encouraged visitors from the States in the early twentieth century. Langston Hughes, with a growing reputation for his poetry about black North America, visited the island and roomed near the Havana railroad station when he escaped a Harlem winter in early 1930. "It seems years since I've felt such warmth or seen such a sky," the twenty-seven-year-old enthused in a letter back to the States. His trip, ostensibly to find a composer using Afro-Cuban rhythms for a folk opera he planned to write, quickly turned into a nonstop literary celebration. Some of his poems had already been translated into Spanish, and he was wined and dined by the black and mulatto literary elite and hailed by the press. With poet Nicolás Guillén he talked about their verse, its tempo, and its negritude. Guillén, one of many who likened Cuba to an alligator for its color and shape, showed to Hughes one of the side effects of a racist society—a strong black and mulatto culture with its own joys and gentry, its own social clubs and fine restaurants, and its own literature. Hughes's residence, Las Villas Hotel and Café, at 20 Avenida de Bélgica, was a five-minute walk from the Club Atenas, where he was fêted by the mulatto elite. ("The dream is a cocktail at Sloppy Joe's," he wrote in his poem "Havana Dreams.")

With the national situation worsening daily, it was still possible to slip in and out of Cuba and absorb its best. As for Hughes, he never found the right musician, but his trip proved beneficial regardless. Hughes was trailed by a low-rent government spy for a while, and "The Little Spy," a short story that first ran in *Esquire*, was the result.

Hughes left just in time. Government repression surfaced to violently quell a nationwide strike against President Gerardo Machado, and the situation deteriorated to mayhem. Ruthless repression, rebellion, reprisals, retaliation, and revolution swept away whatever semblance of order Cuba could claim. Random bombings and mass jailings were common. Hand-tinted postcards from that era show cheerful city strollers buying goods from smiling curbside merchants in spite of the chaos.

Against this backdrop of confusion in Havana's streets, Carleton Beals, a crusading journalist familiar with Latin American politics, visited the island in the fall of 1932. "Beneath the tropical opulence of Cuba, hidden in the tangled jungle of her present cruel political tyranny," he wrote, "are the fangs of bitter discontent. Cuba, unless a remedy is soon found, will be reaped to the holocaust of civil war!" Beals blamed Machado, but he also faulted an American policy toward Cuba that "has helped drive her to despair and ruin."

Beals detailed the situation in *The Crime of Cuba*, and his publisher, Lippincott, wanting photographs to complement the text, asked youthful photographer Walker Evans to spend a couple of weeks on the island with his two cameras. Evans, still a few years away from *Let Us Now Praise Famous Men*, took some four hundred black-and-white photographs, thirty-one of which were printed in Beals's book. He captured the formality of military ceremony, the homeless sleeping on park benches, and common citizens blanketed by the odor of a decaying regime. He stepped inside courtyards and coursed along back streets. Evans's portraits of Havana's washerwomen, newsboys, and dockworkers showed their lives with clarity and dignity. His photos from nearby villages revealed the simplicity and pride of rural life. With his money running out, and evidently bearing a letter of introduction, the twenty-nine-year-old called upon Ernest Hemingway and spent a third week in Cuba at the famous author's expense. His images revealed the habitual activities of daily life that continued unchanged under brutal dictatorships, even one perilously close to its demise. "It was a perplexing job," he wrote Beals upon his return, "so many different courses to follow. I wonder if the illustrations will seem Cuba to you, as you know it."

Cuba was at war, slaughtering itself on a battleground with little direction, no front, and an indeterminate outcome. "Outwardly Havana was a tomb," Beals wrote, "in reality it was a boiling cauldron." Diplomat Sumner Welles, sent to Cuba by newly inaugurated President Franklin D. Roosevelt, began mediation between factions. Havana radio incorrectly announced that Machado had resigned, and thousands of people ran into the streets shouting, "Long live free Cuba!" Machado's forces mowed them down, killing twenty. Walker Evans wrote Carleton Beals: "The old butcher seems firmly in place, still, for some time to come."

The old butcher had to contend with a general strike shutting down industry, transportation, and schools throughout the country. One by one Machado's supporters abandoned him and signed on to the Welles blueprint; when the army did likewise, Machado left for the United States. Welles chose Carlos Manuel de Céspedes as Cuba's provisional president.

After a month, students and army officers, including thirty-two-year-old Sergeant Fulgencio Batista, overthrew de Céspedes in favor of a junta, whose handpicked president, Ramón Grau San Martín, so annoyed the U.S. State Department by unilaterally revoking the 1902 Platt Amendment that it refused to recognize him. Grau's reformist tenure lasted a bit more than four months. It ended with the recently promoted Colonel Batista, now chief of the army, ousting him in favor of two presidents over the next three days. A succession of puppets followed, and finally the two countries agreed to nullify all the provisions of the Platt Amendment except the one allowing the U.S. Navy base at Guantánamo Bay.

While the government was uprooted, below the surface Cuba's colorful life continued. Photographer Rafael Pegudo, for example, staged an exhibit of nudes at Havana's Club Fotográfico, but the gallery's director, described as "a very straight Spaniard," closed it to the public. Many of Pegudo's models were famous prostitutes of the day.

Having been pilloried and sabotaged by foreign governments, and exploited and corrupted by their own, Cubans arrived at a relative calm in 1940 with a new constitution that included enlightened attitudes on elections, public welfare, workers' rights, and civil liberties. Batista, by then a general, put his marionettes away and ran for the presidency himself. Cuban voters, attracted to his progressive platform, gave him a four-year term.

People from the States continued to visit for firsthand observation of the Caribbean's largest island. One such visitor, future monk Thomas Merton, was delighted with his discoveries as he drifted through Cuba in 1940. "Boy, what a place," he said of Havana after watching a flamenco stage show. A father and daughter greeted his bus in a small pueblo with florid songs, composed on the spot, about each passenger. Camagüey was "a swell town, full of cowboys on small horses." Merton sought out priests wherever he went, impressed by their worldliness. He gave an impromptu talk on metaphysics at the central square in Matanzas. A letter home lamented Cuba's prevailing sentiment about blacks: "They won't let them hold big dances in the public squares of small towns."

Foreigners still came by plane and cruise ships for a few days of pricey hedonism and went home happy. Others came to check their considerable manufacturing, mineral, or agricultural subsidiaries. Wealthy Americans with vacation property visited for the sun and warmth. Xanadu, the DuPont estate at Varadero, was so enormous and important that it had its own private customs officer.

Seedy nightclubs, self-important dignitaries, and anti-Batista demonstrations were easy to find, and Constantino Arias photographed them and the city's underclass. A photo essay by Ernesto Fernández showed that fully 90 percent of Havana's lighted storefronts had signs in English. He called his exhibit "La Habana en inglés." When Batista refused to promise free elections, students demonstrated against him. Guerrillas struck at outposts and symbols in the countryside and the cities. Middle-class groups in Havana called for reform. Prostitutes at Guantánamo demanded that sailors pay for their services in weapons, then turned the arms over to revolutionaries.

Fidel's guerrillas struck at Batista's army barracks in Santiago in 1953. Only a handful survived, including Fidel, who was jailed, then in 1955 granted amnesty. He left for Mexico in 1956.

In exile, Fidel Castro, like José Martí seventy-five years earlier, raised money, secured arms, coordinated overseas support, and followed Martí's path through New York and Florida. Back in Mexico City, he met an asthmatic Argentine doctor who had been making his living as a roving photographer. His name was Ernesto Guevara, and he joined up with Fidel, Fidel's younger brother Raúl, and about eighty others in late 1956 for a wind-tossed week-long voyage to Cuba on a secondhand yacht called the *Granma*.

Everything that could go wrong did. An insurrection in Santiago planned to coincide with the *Granma* landing started early and was crushed, the yacht was late and got lost, and no one was there to greet the hapless revolutionary crew when they drifted into swampland in the Gulf of Guacanayabo. No one except tipped-off Batista forces, who quickly killed more than three-quarters of the seasick expeditionaries. Fewer than twenty survivors set out through the Sierra Maestra to topple a dictatorship based on the other end of the island. The Batista government claimed that Castro himself was among the dead.

Photographer Alberto Díaz Gutiérrez, better known as Korda, set up shop in 1956 near the Hotel Capri in the midst of the low-life high rollers who helped give Havana its international reputation for debauchery. Korda's cheesecake photos in the weekly *Carteles* reinforced the capital's sin-city image. His work became so well established that it motivated other photographers to adopt his name—there were "Viejo Korda" and "Genevieve Korda" among others. Korda also inspired the character Códac, the photographer in the terrific *Three Trapped Tigers*.

Meanwhile, back in the Sierra, the amateur army picked up support from peasants who had little to lose. One month after their landing, the ragged guerrilla army, somewhat expanded, overwhelmed a Rural Guard station. They managed to contact urban counterparts and coordinate a supply channel into the mountains.

Herbert Matthews, a correspondent for the *New York Times*, was spirited into Castro's base camp for a clandestine interview. After the first of Matthews's three-part series came out, Batista officials insisted that no reporter could have slipped in and out of the Sierra undetected; and besides, Castro was dead. The next day the *Times* published a photograph of the reporter and his subject at the guerrillas' hideout. From that day forward Fidel Castro seized the mantle of romantic revolutionary.

Less well known but with greater access to the revolutionaries, freelance journalist and photographer Andrew St. George sold pieces about Castro and his cohorts to *Coronet* and other magazines.

During the first week of January 1959, a triumphant Fidel Castro motored westward from the Oriente through small towns toward the capital; photographs show euphoric throngs swarming through the streets, frozen in joyful celebration. It was, wrote photojournalist Lee Lockwood, "one of those rare, magical moments of history when cynics are transformed into romantics and romantics into fanatics."

Castro set up shop in the top floors of the recently opened Havana Hilton while card sharks and croupiers continued to work the first floor. Photographer Korda went from the Hilton's lower levels to its uppermost reaches when Castro picked him as his personal photographer. When the Agrarian Reform Institute, charged with land redistribution, was initiated, veteran photographer Raúl Corral Varela, known as Corrales, was charged with documenting its progress and breakthroughs.

So much took place so quickly in the opening years of the Castro era, and so much of it was highly visible, that anyone with a camera, film, and a trained eye could capture the seismic shifts in progress. Housing, literacy, health care, sports, farming, defense, music, crop harvest, mass media, wages, dairy farming, nationalization, rent control, art, transportation, landownership, education, food distribution—these and dozens of other daily influences went through fundamental change in the revolution's formative period.

In March 1960 a French freighter full of Belgian armaments inexplicably blew up in Havana Harbor, much as the *Maine* had done sixty-two years earlier. The explosion killed one hundred people. The next afternoon Castro again addressed the masses in a speech condemning the United States. It was at this event that photographer Korda snapped his famous photograph of revolutionary Che Guevara. That day Castro introduced ¡*Patria o Muerte!* into the national lexicon, later watered down to ¡*Socialismo o Muerte!*

Castro gave a speech at the United Nations that same year, and the Cuban press entourage accompanying him to New York included *Revolución* editor Carlos Franqui, propagandist of the revolution. In a photograph of the meeting between Fidel Castro and Nikita Khrushchev, their first, Franqui stands anonymously next to the two, a little to the rear. Castro ended up lodging at New York's Hotel Theresa, where a wide range of visitors lined up for a few words with him, including Abdel Nasser, Jawaharlal Nehru, Malcolm X, Allen Ginsberg, and Henri Cartier-Bresson, who took pictures.

Campesinos benefited from the revolution in its first year. Initially landless farmers got individual plots under agrarian reform, a program later expanded and revised in favor of collectivized cultivation over personal ownership. Teachers and health workers anchored themselves in the campo, where neither before had spent much time.

The Cuban government nationalized the United Fruit Company and other American enterprises. As a result, a trade embargo against Cuba was put into place in the waning months of the Eisenhower years. Subsequent presidents tightened and expanded the embargo. Its stated purpose was to prevent trade and commercial development. The real reason, simply put, was to sabotage Cuba's economy and debilitate its leader. Embargo supporters through the years have insisted that it helped Cubans, yet from December 1960 to the present, not one Cuban in a million has benefited by the embargo.

On April 17, 1961, fewer than four months after the United States broke diplomatic relations with Cuba, a force of more than 1,400 Cuban exiles attempted to invade their homeland at the Bay of Pigs on the island's south coast. Their plan was to land at Playa Giron, secure some territory, and provoke enough nationwide chaos to foment a popular uprising against Castro, crippling him and his government until it collapsed. The invaders—trained, financed, and overseen by the Central Intelligence Agency—lost. A few were killed, some escaped, most were captured. Castro took credit for the triumph; President Kennedy accepted blame for the defeat. "Wasn't there anyone around to give you the lecture on Cuba?" Norman Mailer scolded the president afterward. "Don't you sense the enormity of your mistake—you invade a country without understanding its music."

Most of the international coverage of the Bay of Pigs fiasco dwelt on the tactical errors and misplaced confidence of the invaders; very little was said of the maneuvers and strategy of the defenders—in short, it was all why the United States lost rather than how Cuba won. Usually victors write history; in this case they photographed it as well. A picture book by Corrales, *Playa Giron*, holds up as the most revealing work of the conflict and its aftermath. In the midst of the week's turmoil, Castro boasted, "We have made a revolution, a socialist revolution, right here under the very nose of the United States." It was the first time he had publicly acknowledged his revolution's orientation.

The victory at Playa Giron provoked CIA attempts on Castro's life and won Cuba admirers throughout Latin America for beating back the bull. At home it solidified Fidel's dominance. It also provoked irrational policies and odious repression. Orders came from the top for a one-time sweep of Cubans perceived to be too independent of mainstream revolutionary support. Anyone in suddenly sealed-off bohemian sections of Havana and other cities who couldn't produce proper identification was arrested. Armed with lists, authorities sought out, according to Carlos Franqui, "homosexuals, vagrants, suspicious types, intellectuals, artists, Catholics, Protestants, practitioners of voodoo . . . prostitutes and pimps."

Franqui began working on a photographic exhibition of the Cuban revolution, eventually escorting it through a half dozen European and Asian countries. In North Korea, Kim Il Sung ordered the bikinis on mulatto *militianas* covered over.

The October Missile Crisis of 1962 revealed the extremes to which the superpowers would clash in world-threatening one-upmanship. Nuclear missiles, rhetorical bluff, and diplomatic tiptoeing led to a conclusion acceptable to the United States and the Soviet Union.

Cuba, again affronted by two superpowers determining its role, made lots of noise but gained little status.

By this time the Soviet Union had become a firm underwriter of Cuba's economy; Cuba, in return, was a partner on crucial questions of international alliance.

Succeeding U.S. administrations did little to stop—and often encouraged—repeated hit-and-run attacks from air and sea by Cuban exiles. Cuban exile terrorists bombed the country's overseas trade missions as well. The most severe blow, however, came in 1962 when President Kennedy invoked the Trading with the Enemy Act of 1917, which effectively curtailed personal and commercial contact between the two countries.

"Cubans of the militia," Henri Cartier-Bresson noted in mid-1963, "carry rifles the way a tourist carries a camera." The militia, a people's army called up during the victory at Playa Giron, had a strong presence throughout the country. The casinos and porn palaces had been shut down and the prostitutes sent to rehabilitative trade schools. The Havana Hilton became the Habana Libre. "It is as if the Amish had taken over Las Vegas," lamented Kenneth Tynan in *Holiday* magazine. Cartier-Bresson called it "a pleasure island that has gone adrift," adding, "the people are easygoing and full of humor and kindness and grace, but . . . nobody will easily convert them into hard Communist zealots."

By the late 1960s Carlos Franqui, Fidel's compañero from the Sierra Maestra, had moved to Europe and denounced the regime he once served. Castro used photographic technology to retaliate: whenever that picture of Castro and Khrushchev at the United Nations has appeared in Cuba, Franqui has been airbrushed out, photographically disappeared. Huber Matos, another comrade from the early days who was imprisoned for twenty years for questioning the revolution's direction, was likewise airbrushed from history. He has been disappeared from domestically published photographs of triumphant guerrillas entering Havana in January 1959.

During the Jimmy Carter years Washington and Havana exchanged low-level diplomatic missions, the closest the countries had come to recognition in more than fifteen years. By the end of Carter's administration there were commercial flights to Cuba. That didn't last long.

On April Fool's Day 1980, twelve Cubans crashed a minivan through the gates of the Peruvian embassy in Havana seeking asylum. Within days thousands of others joined them, and soon Cuba made a strategic decision: anyone who wanted to leave the country could. The rest of that spring and through the summer hundreds of boats of all sizes and horsepowers arrived from the States at the port of Mariel west of Havana, and Cubans, unsure of their fate, crowded on board for the ninety-mile ride to Key West. Families had to make immediate decisions that would affect the rest of their lives. Some prepared to abandon their *patria* only to unpack at the last minute. Others were coerced to leave because they were prisoners or considered counterrevolutionary. One divorced parent could prevent the other from departing if children were involved. "Did you hear? Pedro left, but Myrna and the kids stayed." "*Oye*, Carlos cried all night when Carlitos announced he was going." The fiery subject burned through Cuba's consciousness during the sweltering summer of Mariel. Despite the scorn heaped on the *émigrés* in mass progovernment street demonstrations and by Cuban bureaucrats handling the departures, fully 125,000 Cubans chose to leave their own country before the program wound down 5 months later. Needless to say, the unexpected influx of "undesirables" adversely affected Jimmy Carter's reelection bid.

―――

"You gave all of us who are alone in this country," Norman Mailer wrote Castro at the time of the revolution, "some sense that there were heroes left in the world." To some that image had been indelibly stained, yet Castro's Cuba at the beginning of the 1980s remained enormously popular throughout most of Latin America as the symbol of a developing smaller nation successfully standing up to an overdeveloped larger one. Cuba's qualities couldn't be quantified—municipal bands in small-town plazas; fine, dark sand on south coast beaches; sunset along the Malecón; and tobacco leaves maturing under cheesecloth in the Viñales Valley. The international self-respect that Cuba had carefully nourished spilled over to its citizens with an intrinsic sense of dignity and egalitarianism far wider than in previous regimes. But you still couldn't find a newsstand anywhere in the country.

Post-Mariel Cuba continued much as before. The country's commercial output increased slightly, but it was most proud of its sophisticated biotechnical industry coupled with advanced research in pharmaceuticals.

Silvio Rodríguez and Pablo Milanes earned international followings with their soft ballads of personal optimism. The country's movie industry brought out films over the years such as *Memories of Underdevelopment* (1973) and *La Bella del Alhambre* (1989); the reputation of its annual international film festival grew throughout the Americas. Cuban baseball and boxing continued to excel in international competition. Although some of its more notable writers left the country, Cuba still maintained a productive literary output, its community of writers publishing what and where they could. Painters and other artists stretched their limited resources to bring out widely interpretive modern and postmodern contemporary works.

In 1985 the American government began broadcasting a station called Radio Martí, aimed exclusively at Cubans on the island. Despite its lack of credibility, Radio Martí grew to become a principal in the propaganda war between countries. In 1989, on their own state media, Cubans were riveted by the sensational drug trial of ranking officials, best known among them being the highly decorated and highly regarded General Arnaldo Ochoa. Ochoa was convicted of smuggling and hastily executed along with three others. Many Cubans started to question their own leadership.

Two months before Radio Martí began broadcasting, Mikhail Gorbachev assumed power in Moscow. He soon became the toast of the Western world, which led Castro to observe that the Russian's reforms, if successful, "will be good for socialism and everyone else." If not, he predicted, "the consequences will be especially hard for us."

The consequences were especially hard for them. In the spring of 1989, 88 percent of Cuba's trade came from Warsaw Pact countries. Within a few years there were no Warsaw Pact nations left to trade with. Cuba almost capsized. Its athletes were the only winners in those difficult years.

Cuba managed to stay afloat while its former Eastern European allies sank because, in part, Castro had come to power as a popular leader, not a promoted apparatchik. His leadership, which many outside the country saw as tenuous, from inside appeared unassailable. The reservoir of loyalty and affection he built up over the years, especially in the Oriente, had not yet drained below the danger mark. Long guilty of leaning on other countries for its support, the nation began a long period of painful and strenuous readjustment. Cuba was finally, after some ninety years, independent.

In 1990 Castro proclaimed his country's economic free-fall the "Special Period in a Time of Peace." The following decade was devastating for Cubans who had accustomed themselves to a higher standard of living. The country could buy almost nothing, including petroleum from overseas. Cubans were forced to improvise spare parts for machinery, and anything that required petroleum to operate— vehicles, elevators, power stations, water pumps, farm and industrial machinery—was reduced or eliminated. Most cars were put up on blocks, replaced by bicycles.

The sugar harvests declined, plagued by unseasonably awful weather and broken-down equipment. The domestic economy had been mugged by the black market, where everything was available at wildly fluctuating prices—provisions, matches, clothing, perfume, cigarettes, gasoline. A majority of Havana's work centers stopped operating entirely. Daily blackouts of up to eight or more hours meant no lights, no pump to bring water to upper floors, food spoiling in room-temperature refrigerators. Cubans were admonished to listen to the radio rather than watch television because it used less electricity. The ration book that awarded each household in the country a certain amount of fish or meat monthly meant little; entitlement didn't mean availability. A television cooking show featuring banana skin picadillo was taken off the air after more than forty years. Air conditioning was just a rumor. The underground economy's Wall Street rose along the Malecón, manipulated by *bisneros*. Prostitution rose along with male tourism from Mexico, Italy, and elsewhere. Petty crime surfaced. "How is a Cuban like a seal?" a friend asked with a glint in his eye and a hand to his ears. "Because he's up to here underwater and he's still clapping."

The Special Period now seemed less special and more normal. "To return to capitalism would be a step backward in history," Castro warned his countrymen in 1991. Two years later he took a couple of tentative steps in that direction by decriminalizing the possession of foreign currency in the hands of Cubans. Giddy Cubans ran through the streets clutching dollar bills they had stashed under their flimsy mattresses. The alligator's economy, then near a standstill, began to creak and groan into motion.

Instead of clapping, though, many Cubans set out northward from the island in homemade rafts; by the summer of 1994 the flotilla reached the thousands, and the Castro government did nothing to prevent it. A rare public antigovernment demonstration took place that same summer in crowded Centro Habana. Fidel himself showed up, waded through the hostile crowd, talked with a few demonstrators, then got in a car and left. In Washington, Congress passed the Cuban Adjustment Act that allowed newly arrived Cubans a clear passage to a green card and citizenship. Later the law was modified to include the "wet-foot dry-foot" policy—a Cuban need merely touch U.S. soil to be allowed on the path to eventual citizenship. If, on the other hand, the Coast Guard caught Cubans at sea, they were turned away. No other country's citizens enjoyed such a privilege. It lasted until early 2017.

The most wrenching circumstance mixing policy, politics, and family took place in late 1999 when a five-year-old Cuban boy accompanied his mother and many others headed to America on a motorized craft. His father, back home in Cárdenas, knew nothing of this. The boat capsized in the waters east of Florida and all but Elián González and two others drowned, including his mother. He was placed in the custody of relatives in Miami and soon personified the tug-of-war between Cuban Americans, on one hand, and the rest of America, on the other. The Elián González case became America's daily topic—from the corner water cooler to late-night comedy monologues to a *New Yorker* cartoon. The international brouhaha provided Cuba ready-made propaganda. I saw Elián's two grandmothers, having just returned from visiting him in Miami, ride slowly, parade-style down the Malecón in convertibles, smiling and waving to anyone who looked like they would smile and wave back. In April 2000 the Clinton Justice Department seized Elián from the home of his recalcitrant relative and reunited him with his welcoming father. Most of the American public, the Cuban government, and Elián himself approved of the results.

For some, the Special Period had no end. Rationing continued, yet combined with the monthly government wage of about twenty-five dollars it supplied enough food for only three weeks. You were on your own for the fourth week, and that's where the black market came in.

A few years into the Special Period, a change of policy allowed artists and musicians to keep most of their earnings, domestic and foreign, instead of turning them over to the government. Soon the cultural world was an industry unto itself with creators, agents, curators, publicists, and salesmen. Buyers from around the world came to Havana art galleries and showrooms, dropped thousands of dollars, and went home pleased.

Eventually—and tepidly—the government encouraged Cubans to open small businesses of their own, and in 2010 released a list of more than two hundred "Legalized Self-Employment Occupations." Among the professions: mechanical saw operator, babysitter, record and CD seller, breeder of pets, book binder, photographer, bus stop barker ("calls out instructions to waiting passengers"), makeup artist, parking lot attendant, piñata maker, mattress repair service, translator, car body remolder, real estate broker, and "women who pose for tourists wearing colorful colonial attire." Many of these professions were already in service, but now they were codified. Inexpensive petroleum shipments from friendly Venezuela allowed the nation's machinery to continue pumping, with the excess resold in the international marketplace.

━━━

"I had cautioned myself against any undue romantic persuasion," LeRoi Jones (later Amiri Baraka) wrote when he visited Cuba in 1960. His was a well-advised warning, and it is one that first-time travelers through the island should take to heart today. It allows you to appreciate the country on its own terms and on no one else's. Some call it the Columbus syndrome, in which first-time visitors ooh and aah at the island's friendliness and beauty, then, back home, gush about it as if they were the first to explore it. Like LeRoi Jones, I too had cautioned myself against any undue persuasion.

In those days the Miami airport assigned the Havana charter the latest flight time and the farthest distance from the ticket counter. They loved to watch us stand in line for hours. Finally, around 2 a.m., we were allowed to board our charter for the 225-mile flight to Havana. We did not sing "Kumbaya." When, forty-five minutes later we were circling over the lights of Havana, we cheered. Our cheers stopped abruptly when the pilot told us that Jose Martí airport was too fogged in to land and we would have to head back to Miami and start all over again the next morning. The more conspiracy minded among us saw a plot to sabotage the American left. Others among us assumed the pilot knew what he was doing. Eventually we landed at Havana late the following morning. A few passengers broke into "Guantanamera." For a number of years I visited the island for family, magazine assignments, and research projects. By the end of the century I felt confident enough, with a colleague, to set up bilingual writing workshops for American and Cubans together—fiction, nonfiction, poetry, playwriting, performance art, translation, and travel writing. We pulled it off for two years, but as we were preparing for the third year the U.S. government yanked our license and the Cuban authorities refused us their facilities. We said, well, if neither of them wants us, to hell with it, and so ended our noble binational literary experiment.

But still, there was this gnawing feeling that Cuba's literary life— overground, underground, all flavors—should be exposed to foreigners. So for the next decade or so I led Americans (and one South African) on Literary Havana tours. The itinerary included the obvious—the Hemingway Museum, the secondhand book dealers at the Plaza de Armas, the town of Regla, and Afro-Cuban art at Callejón Hamel. And the not so obvious—a stroll through Barrio Chino to its senior citizens center, Ediciones Vigía, a publishing house in Matanzas, a morning with a drama ensemble at the Bertolt Brecht Theater, a visit to the Jewish community center, and most of all, an afternoon at the fourth-floor walk-up home of internationally acclaimed poet Reina María Rodríguez. If you looked over the edge of her *azotea* (rooftop) you'd see the friendly slums of Centro Havana. Through the Special Period, Reina would invite poets and translators to her azotea for a literary mixer. They read, they wrote, they published, they composed, they defected, abandoning Cuba for other lands. During one visit a hush fell over the azotea and Reina read a poem from a bilingual anthology. Then, as if choreographed, one of our group—an FM classical music deejay—calmly took the book and flawlessly read the same poem in English, as if he was intimately familiar with it. There was applause on the rooftop when he finished, and finally Reina spoke: "Now this is what poetry is supposed to be."

It turns out Fidel Castro was not infallible. In the first decade of the new century he fell from a platform, shattering a kneecap and breaking an arm. He later suffered from gastrointestinal bleeding for which repeated surgeries were required. In 2006 his younger brother Raúl, head of the armed forces and with a very different personal administrative style, took over the temporary reins of government. Two years later, his health no better, Fidel officially resigned his myriad posts, giving Raúl his full power and his blessing. Except for a sporadic column in the country's Communist Party newspaper or an occasional photo with a visiting dignitary, Fidel drifted out of sight—though he continued to entertain Venezuelan president Hugo Chávez, who visited Cuba for cancer treatments.

Raúl, meanwhile, took part in back-door diplomacy with the United States facilitated by Pope Francis. The result was thunder and lightning on December 17, 2014, when President Raúl Castro and President Barack Obama announced their intentions to renew diplomatic relations after more than five decades of brooding, suspicion, and bitter animosity. In March 2016 President Obama visited the island to deliver a speech of friendship. That same week a Major League baseball team played the Cuban national team before a capacity crowd at Havana's Latinoamericano Stadium. The week ended with the Rolling Stones performing a free outdoor concert for a delirious audience of half a million. Obama was wildly popular, much to the distress of government hard-liners.

Fidel Castro, who nurtured and guided his country for almost half a century, did not hear his name mentioned once that wonderful week—not to credit, not even to recognize. You could imagine him mumbling in his sickbed, "What do they think I am, chopped chorizo?"

All three events—Obama's visit, Major League baseball, and the Rolling Stones—were enthusiastically received. The alligator started to stir.

SOURCES

Auster, Paul. *In the Country of Last Things.* New York: Viking, 1987.

Beals, Carleton. *The Crime of Cuba.* New York: Lippincott, 1933.

Cartier-Bresson, Henri. "An Island of Pleasure Gone Adrift." *Life,* March 16, 1963.

Fuentes, Norberto. *The Autobiography of Fidel Castro.* Trans. Anna Kushner. New York: W. W. Norton, 2010.

Leech, Margaret. *In the Days of McKinley.* New York: Harper, 1959.

Lockwood, Lee. *Castro's Cuba: An American Journalist's Inside Look at Cuba 1959–1969.* New York: Vintage Books, 1969.

Matthews, Herbert L. "Cuban Rebel Is Visited in Hideout." *New York Times,* February 24, 1957.

Miller, Tom. *Trading with the Enemy: A Yankee Travels Through Castro's Cuba.* New York: Atheneum, 1992.

Miller, Tom, ed. *Travelers' Tales—Cuba.* San Francisco: Travelers' Tales, 2004.

Thomas, Hugh. *Cuba: A History.* New York: Penguin, 2010.

CREDITS

"Cubana Be/Cubana Bop" contains material from *Traveler's Tales—Cuba*; the interview with Omara Portuondo first appeared in the *Los Angeles Times*. "On the Street" includes material from the *Washington Post, Las Vegas Life* (August 1999), the program for the New Orleans by the Bay festival (June 1997), and *Mungo Park*. The chapter "The Streets of 1898" was originally published as "Remember the Maine" from *Smithsonian* magazine (February 1998). The chapter "Third Gear" was originally published as "Old Cars in Cuba: Nurtured but Not Loved" in the *New York Times* and is reprinted here by permission. Parts of "These Three Kings" were originally published in the *Washington Post* and the *Los Angeles Times*. Parts of "Las Parrandas" were originally published in "Season of Las Parrandas" in *Natural History* (December—January 1997–98), copyright © Natural History Magazine, Inc., 1997. Material about José Martí ran first in *WorldView* (fall 1996); and the *Washington Post* first printed the material about Fidel Castro's faux autobiography and my purchase of the famous picture of Che Guevara from the photographer. Most of the Hemingway material came from *Mungo Park*, except for my account of receiving the 1954 Nobel Prize for Literature, which the *Los Angeles Times* first ran. Parts of "Undue Romantic Persuasion" ran in *Life* magazine as well as the introduction to *Cuba*, photographs by Adam Kufeld (W. W. Norton, 1994). All of the above-cited works are reprinted by permission.

INDEX

ABOUT THE AUTHOR

Tom Miller has been writing about Latin America and the American Southwest for more than forty years, bringing us extraordinary stories of ordinary people. Miller's highly acclaimed adventure books include *The Panama Hat Trail* about South America; *On the Border*, an account of his travels along the U.S.-Mexico frontier; *Trading with the Enemy*, which takes readers on his journeys through Cuba; and, about the American Southwest, *Revenge of the Saguaro*. Additionally, he has edited three compilations: *How I Learned English*, *Travelers' Tales Cuba*, and *Writing on the Edge: A Borderlands Reader*. Miller has appeared in *Smithsonian*, the *New Yorker*, *LIFE*, the *New York Times*, the *Washington Post*, the *Los Angeles Times*, *Natural History*, and many other publications. He wrote the introduction to *Best Travel Writing*—2005, and leads educational tours in and around Cuba. Visit his website at TomMillerBooks.com.